THE WOMEN WHO CHANGED THE COURSE OF HISTORY

Eve, Cleopatra, Isabel the Catholic, Marie Curie, Winnie Mandela, Benazir Bhutto & Juana Azurduy. Lessons from the Great Women that Forged our Society.

- SECOND EDITION -

By Dominique Atkinson

© *Copyright 2015*

DISCLAIMER

Note from the Author:

Destiny is both unpredictable and fickle. Eva, Juana Azurduy, Isabella the Catholic, Marie Curie, Winnie Mandela, Hillary Rodham Clinton, and Benazir Bhutto: all women whose lives changed the course of history. They would have been remarkable in any era in which they were born. But by living when they did, each defined the times in which they lived. Their actions transformed the imprint of their countries and the world.

Eve, the prototype for the female gender, got things off to a bad start. Condemned by the male power structure for millennia following Eve's surrender to temptation, the fair sex received generations of unfair treatment based upon Eve's error in judgment. The fact that Adam was just as guilty managed to get a pass as authority was deemed the destiny of males because women had proven themselves weak and flawed. Women were expected to know their place, to accept their subjugation to the husbands and fathers who were given authority over them, and to obey without question. When, throughout history, women emerged from obscurity to take their place in government, science, struggles for liberty, the arts, or other arenas

3

where they were expected to remain spectators and not performers, they were judged by a set of standards that regarded their gender as more important than their achievements.

When they succeeded, as Cleopatra did in defending her realm, Isabella the Catholic did in ruling Castile, or Victoria did in reigning over an empire, they challenged the preconceived notions that believed a male would have done a better job. When they were trailblazers, as Marie Curie was in science, Mary Wollstonecraft in writing, Benazir Bhutto and Hillary Rodham Clinton in politics, Winnie Mandela in activism, and Juana Azurduy in battle, they fought two conflicts: one to achieve their goals, the other against a power structure that would value a man's accomplishments over a woman's. They endured condemnation, hostility, scorn, poverty, violence, and even death in their crusade to achieve their goals, but they did not capitulate. None of them expected the road to be an easy one; they'd been women all their lives and they knew, going in, that the path was an uphill climb.

The women in the following chapters are females who excelled in what is often called a man's world. But thanks to their efforts as well as their sacrifices, the daughters of Eve have found that it was meant to be their world, too. If any of these women were to be taken out of history's record, the ensuing gap would be enormous. All of these women raise questions about what it is to live a life so fully, for there can be no doubt that these women held nothing back. Not for them a half-hearted existence; they poured everything they had into their endeavors.

Let's get to know them!

Best,

Dominique Atkinson

Table of Contents

Eve the Mother of All

Who was Eve?

According to the three monotheistic religions Judaism, Christianity, and Islam, Eve was the first woman in God's creation, the world's introduction to the female gender of the human species. Her story is told in the Book of Genesis, the first book in the Old Testament, which is also part of the Christian Bible. Genesis relates the tale of an earthly paradise known as Eden, created by God, as a home to the first man, Adam.

In a perfect and pristine world, Adam enjoyed all the beauty that Nature could provide for his pleasure. Well, almost all of it. God had instructed his human creation that he could eat from any tree in the Garden, except for one: if he ate from the tree of knowledge of good and evil, he would die. But with so many other trees available, surely it was easy enough to abstain from the fruit of one lone tree. Apparently it was for Adam, as Genesis makes no mention of the first man displaying any untoward interest in what God had told him to avoid.

10

Adam's task was to name the animals, and to work the Garden of Eden and care for it. In the early days, the tasks seemed easy enough; no back-breaking effort, no sweat of his brow. But God recognized that while labor was plentiful, staffing was limited and companionship absent. God said, "It is not good for the man to be alone. I will make a helper suitable for him." Adam had been created from the dust of Eden, and he received the breath of life from God. Creating a female seems to have required a little more finesse and some surgical skill; while Adam was in a deep sleep, God operated on him, removing one of his ribs and then closing up the incision. From that rib, the woman was created. Adam, upon waking, met his mate and was pleased with what he saw, and the pair seemed destined for happily ever after.

In the Beginning

But maybe Adam was so busy naming the birds of the air and the beasts of the ground that he had neglected to thoroughly instruct the woman in God's "Thou shalt nots." When the wily serpent, bent on mischief, approached Eve, he was able to persuade her that eating from the tree of the knowledge of good and evil would do no harm. It would simply broaden her skill set so that, like God, she would be able to discern right from wrong. What could be bad about that? If she had never paid much attention to the tree before, seeing it from the serpent's perspective made the fruit suddenly appear so much more appetizing.

Intent on a learning experience, the woman bit into what has become known as the forbidden fruit. Genesis doesn't identify the fruit which was produced by the tree of the knowledge of good and evil, but for millennia, scholars and theologians have been transfixed with curiosity. The most popular selection is an apple, supported by the theory that the reason the male larynx, or Adam's apple, is so prominent is because the fruit got stuck in Adam's throat when he tried to swallow it. But there's more than one candidate for the title of forbidden fruit. When painting the scene upon the ceiling of the Sistine Chapel, Renaissance artist Michelangelo chose the fig.

Genesis does not name the fruit that was destined to stir up so much difficulty. The woman found it tasty, and being a good wife, she shared it with her husband. The fruit lived up to the hype, because immediately upon sampling it, husband and wife, who had previously lived in a state of unclad innocence, noticed that they were naked. They swiftly worked to repair the absence of clothes by stitching garments for themselves out of fig leaves.

Early Influences

When God, as was his habit, came to visit them in the cool of the day, they remained hidden from him. God asked them where they were. Adam replied that they didn't want to show themselves before God, because they were naked. God, just like a parent who already knows the answer before the children have had a chance to concoct an alibi, asked, "Who told you that you're naked?" Followed by "Have you eaten from the tree you were told not to eat from?"

Adam would have failed a marriage encounter test; he immediately blamed the woman and by implication, God, when he said that the woman (that God put in the Garden with him) gave him the fruit from the tree, and he ate it. The woman was just as swift in passing

13

on the blame; lacking a human cause for her act, she accused the serpent of deceiving her.

Although history knows her as Eve, the first woman actually had three names. She was initially known as "woman" but that's more of a title rather than a name. Later in Genesis, both are referred to as Adam; one name for the two who become one flesh. She receives her constant name of Eve after the cataclysmic events that follow the expulsion from Eden.

Eve's Life Changes
Paradise was no longer home for Adam and his mate. Her punishment would be painful childbirth and subjugation to her husband, an indication that in the perfect world that Eden was originally designed to be, marriage was based on equality and children would arrive effortlessly and without labor pains. Adam's punishment condemned him to the hardship of a life where agriculture resisted conquest; the very ground was cursed because of him, and the soil would not easily give up its fruits. Work would be rigorous and demanding, and the soil that produced his food would do double duty as the eternal resting place of men and

women, now mortal and condemned to return to the dust from which Adam had been made.

After God cursed them, Adam gave his wife a name; until this point, she was referred to as "the woman." It's after learning her fate that she receives the name of Eve from Adam, because she would become the mother of mankind. God sewed clothing for them out of skins, certainly more durable than fig leaves, and then they were banished east of Eden.

Tragedy haunted the first man and woman. Their eldest son Cain killed their second son Abel, introducing murder into the world. Adam went silent after his final conversation with God before the eternal exile from Eden; the Old Testament records no further words from Adam. But Eve continued the dialogue and surprisingly, her words are optimistic. When she gave birth to her first child, she praised God for his help in the delivery. When she bore another son, Seth, after Abel is murdered, she acknowledged God's gift. The nuances show a woman who came to terms with her punishment. Later, in the New Testament, the Book of Matthew traces Jesus' lineage through Seth, the son who was a gift from God to replace the son she lost.

But Eve, along with the women who followed her, paid dearly for her transgression, and in the eyes of the church, she was responsible for the fall from grace. After all, it was Eve who fell for the serpent's lies, and church scholars from Paul to Tertullian to Bernard of Clairvaux blamed her for her sin. In the view of the medieval church, Eve tempted Adam into disobedience and the lesson was clear: women could not be trusted. They were weak, sinful, seductive and easily swayed. When validation was needed for why men held higher status in society, with women regarded as inferior beings, the answer was clear to any churchgoer. Genesis indicted her. The Bible made its case against Eve and she was judged guilty.

Medieval and Renaissance art, recognizing an alluring subject for their paintings, sided with the church fathers. She was seen as a seductress, plying her feminine wiles as Adam helplessly succumbs to her blandishments, although the account in Genesis does not cast her in that light. Eve as the gateway to sin was a popular interpretation of the ancient story; religious

16

art was the teaching tool of its time and men and women who could not read could interpret the images before them. Beware of women; they lead to hell.

Why Eve Matters

Eve appears at the dawn of creation, long before concepts of gender equality, misogyny, discrimination, and equal rights would be voiced. For thousands of years, Eve's sin cast a long shadow over her gender, and the daughters of Eve were consigned to inferior status as payment for her transgression. The patriarchal society found it easy to use the Bible as justification for the subjugation of women, but that doesn't mean that females were predestined to occupy lower status. The Old and New Testaments, as well as early church history, identify women who occupied positions of power and influence in a society that was dominated by men. The Bible was written by men, and church history was dominated by men; women were kept in their place because Eve's sin had deep roots.

Judaism, the mother ship for the vessel that would become Christianity, shared many tenets with its religious offspring, but as the followers of Christ evolved from a sect into a separate religion, the leaders absorbed the Old Testament into their holy books but did not necessarily interpret the message in the same way. Jews did not believe in original sin, but for Christians, the sin of disobedience was responsible for introducing death to the human race. While Adam is indicted for the downfall of mankind, the early church fathers lost little time in placing the blame upon Eve. Following the Fall, women came with a warning label, destined to be denied positions of power and equality because of the Eden experience. In the New Testament, Paul, whose writings formed the foundation of Christian theology, made his case for barring women from stature in church leadership. The explanation in I Timothy 2 orders women to be silent in church. "For Adam was formed first, then Eve, and Adam was not deceived, but the woman was deceived and became a transgressor." Her salvation could only come through childbirth, provided that labor pains were accompanied by faith, love, and holiness. There was a caveat: the childbirth had to be accompanied by modesty. Yet in his other writings, Paul credited the women who supported his ministry and displayed their faith, so it's hard to categorically assert that he was hostile to women.

That appreciation would not carry through the

18

subsequent generations. The Bishop Augustine, later Saint, of Hippo, lived from 354-430 AD, wrote, "It is still Eve the temptress that we must beware of in any woman . . . I fail to see what use woman can be o man, if one excludes the function of bearing children." Tertullian wrote of the female gender, "And do you not know that you are Eve? God's sentence hangs still over all your sex and His punishment weights down upon you. You are the devil's gateway." Tertullian certainly had a way with imagery. Woman, he denounced, "is a temple build over a sewer." The passage of time failed to ease the judgment imposed upon females by the male church fathers. Protestant leader John Calvin, wrote, "Thus the woman . . . is forced back to her own position. She had, indeed, previously been subject to her husband, but that was a liberal and gentle subjection; now, however, she is cast into servitude."

To the church leaders, Eve began her existence in a state of subordination because God created Adam on his own, but created Eve from Adam's rib. Not only was she inferior in authority but she had proven herself inferior in judgment. Adam desired her just as men would continue to desire women, but that was not because of a natural physical need for one another. No, it was because women were temptresses who used their wiles on men.

19

What it does mean is that women had more barriers to overcome when seeking greater independence in their lives. Although the Old Testament shows that Deborah was a wise and effective judge in Old Testament Israel, women would have to battle stereotypes and preconceived ideas about their abilities before they would be allowed to vote, be elected to office, and even in many cases learn to read and write. Queen Elizabeth I ruled England with a level of skill and ability that rivaled any of England's kings, but it was only in this century that the firstborn child of the heir to the British throne would become next in line, regardless of gender. Had Princess Charlotte beaten Prince George to the firstborn punch, England would one day see the coronation of Queen Charlotte.

Maintaining women as second-class citizens is not exclusive to believers in the Judeo-Christian tradition. Although there have been, throughout history, matriarchal societies where power was invested in females, that's the exception rather than the rule. In order to evaluate Eve's legacy apart from the generations who came after her and wore the fetters of inferiority because of her, it's necessary to see her as she was written. Banishment from Eden, painful childbirth and being ruled by her husband were all part of her sentence. But Eve's resilience kept her in communication with God when Adam opted for silence, his conversation ending by blaming Eve for giving him the fruit that he ate. He gave his wife a name, and from then on had nothing noteworthy for Genesis to record.

She was an irresistible subject for writers, and as women took to their pens, they evaluated the mother of them all thoughtfully. *Eve's Apology in Defense of Women*, written during the Renaissance by Aemilia Lanyer, uses Pilate's wife to speak on behalf of the First Woman. Eve, Pilate's wife explains, simply tasted the fruit, enjoyed it, and shared it with no awareness of what the consequences would be. God's failure to be specific, Adam's lack of detail, left Eve as merely curious, not malicious. Rachel Speght, writing in 1617, makes the assertion that because Eve was created from Adam's rib, she was his equal and not his inferior; Adam, after all, was made from dust. Perhaps Speght perceived the irony that it fell to women, the wielder of brooms and cleaning, to sweep up the makings of the first husband as a household task. Or perhaps she keenly felt the ostracism of her gender. Poet Christina Rossetti, evoked Eve's mourning and her own guilt in the death of one son at the hands of the other; Eve was still viewed as culpable, but she was seen sympathetically.

It's worth noting that Eve may have been damned by Christianity's early theologians and writers, but she came off rather well in the hands of Mark Twain, who wrote *Eve's Diary,* believed by many have been inspired by his love for his wife who died recently. Eve's appreciation of beauty and her fascination with the natural world are seen as admirable. Upon her death, Adam says, "Wherever she was, there was Eden."

Cleopatra VII the Pharaoh of Egypt 69-30 BC

Who was Cleopatra VII?

Cleopatra VII, one of history's most famous queens, has been immortalized in cinema and literature. Femme fatale Elizabeth Taylor played her in the movie rendition of Cleopatra's life, a film which became as much of a scandal as the romances of the Egyptian queen herself when Taylor and Richard Burton, playing the part of Mark Antony, took their love affair off camera. Shakespeare in his play Antony and Cleopatra wrote of her, "Age cannot wither her, nor custom stale, her infinite variety." George Bernard Shaw in his play Caesar and Cleopatra draws on the story of the young Cleopatra and the seasoned Roman. The woman herself risks being lost behind the legend that has intrigued the imagination of civilization.

In the Beginning

The dynasty which began with Ptolemy, one of Alexander the Great's generals, who claimed Egypt as his conquest after Alexander's death divided his empire, would end with Cleopatra VII. Ptolemy was a Macedonian, a comrade and perhaps, if rumors were true, the half-brother of Alexander the Great. If it's true that Ptolemy was the illegitimate son of Philip II, he would have brought royal blood to the Egyptian throne. Ptolemy showed a flair for combat and a decided talent for attracting attention: when the Persian king Darius III, who was defeated by Alexander, was later assassinated, Ptolemy tracked the assassin down and returned him to Alexander wearing nothing but chains and a dog collar.

Alexander conquered every country in his path, but when he died, his vast empire was divided among his generals. Ptolemy won Egypt in the geographic lottery. Ptolemy didn't go to his new kingdom empty-handed; he stole the body of Alexander while it was returning to Macedonia. Ptolemy proved to be an effective rule, establishing a solid financial and administrative foundation. He later moved the capital of the nation to Alexandria, partly to avoid the influence of the priests in Memphis and partly because Alexandria was closer to his homeland.

The dynasty was heavily influenced by Greece, and the royal family spoke Greek as an official language. Ptolemy made Alexandria a center of learning; the library attracted scholars of renown including Euclid and Archimedes. The lighthouse, Pharos, would be named one of the seven wonders of the ancient world. Ptolemy's dynasty, with its Greek influences, would last for nearly three hundred years, defeated only when Julius Caesar was triumphant over the Egyptians. But Rome would find itself entranced by the allure of the female pharaoh, the last of the line.

The Egyptians were a brilliant civilization, but their rulers seemed to lack a basic awareness of family dynamics. The Egyptian throne was often shared, and as a result, murder frequently resulted, because siblings and power sharing are rarely compatible whether the sharing is done by commoners or pedigreed royals. Egyptian tradition required that a woman could not rule as the sole monarch; she required a male consort. Cleopatra was the co-ruler of Egypt first with her father, and then with her brothers, who were also her husbands, in accordance with Egyptian custom.

When her father, Ptolemy XII died in 51 BCE, he left the throne to his ten-year old son Ptolemy XII and his 18-year old daughter, Cleopatra. Egyptian tradition must have been extraordinarily optimistic to think that this was a viable pattern of government. Cleopatra did not include her brother/husband in the coinage, appearing solo on the coins and thus asserting her supremacy in one of the most tangible ways she could. Cleopatra, who presented herself as the reincarnation of Isis, the quintessential female goddess whose domain of marriage, fertility, and motherhood made her one of the ranking deities in the pantheon, actually learned to speak Egyptian, the language of the people she ruled. Her linguistic skills were impressive and effective; her fluency in Egyptian, Greek, and other languages meant that she didn't need a translator when she was negotiating with the diplomats from other countries. Not long after becoming the pharaoh, she dispensed with counsel from her advisors and made her own decisions on state matters. According to Plutarch, her very voice was like "an instrument of many strings." The advisors may have thought otherwise.

But she ran afoul of the Roman troops known as the Gabiniani, who had murdered the sons of the governor of Syria, a Roman named Marcus Calpurnius Bibulus, and Cleopatra turned the Gabiniani in to the governor. Their enmity contributed to Cleopatra's fall; two of her officials overthrew her and placed her brother Ptolemy XIII on the throne because he would be easier to control than his sister. Cleopatra, accompanied by her half-sister Arsinoe, fled into exile.

Egypt was not the only nation in the throes of internal warfare. Rome was also wracked by civil war. Pompey, who had been appointed as the Roman guardian for the younger members of the Ptolemy family and had spent a lot of time in Egypt, fled to the country after his defeat at Pharsalus by Julius Caesar. If he had counted on sentiment to rescue him, he was fatally disappointed.

At age 13, Ptolemy XIII was unschooled in the ways of politics. In order to please the powerful Roman Julius Caesar, it's believed that the young pharaoh ordered the beheading of Pompey, once part of the First Triumvirate with Caesar until they ended up on

27

opposite sides of a civil war. While offering a potential ally the severed head of his enemy might seem like a good tactic, it turned out to be a mistake. Caesar was not pleased. He declared Egypt to be under martial law, took over the capital city of Alexandria and decreed that he would judge the two claimants to the Egyptian throne. The boy-king and his court fled to Pelusium, but Caesar had him brought back to the capital.

Early Influences

Cleopatra's life, had it not been lived by a real person, would have suited fiction just as well. Her earliest influences would include the crown-or-be-killed game plan of Egyptian politics, so from her youth she had to adapt to the survival-of-the-fittest ruling strategy. But she was a quick learner, and she figured out early on that in order to hold power, she needed powerful allies.

Monarchs in the ancient world didn't have the benefit of press agents or publicity managers or spin doctors, but Cleopatra was more than effective at generating her own P.R. In 47 BCE, still living in exile but determined to make an impression on Rome's most illustrious celebrity, Cleopatra had herself rolled up in a carpet and brought into the palace to meet Caesar. It was a logical move: he was effective, he was influential, and he was male. The meeting must have gone well; within nine months, she gave birth to Ptolemy Caesar, more commonly known as Caesarion. Caesar supported his mistress' claim to the Egyptian throne but establishing her rule was not going to be so simple. Her half-sister Arsinoe took the throne and had herself named as queen. Cleopatra and her Roman lover had to wait six months for reinforcements from Rome; when the troops arrived, the Romans defeated young Ptolemy's army in battle. Ptolemy XIII drowned in the Nile when he was trying to escape. Ptolemy's supporters either died in battle or soon afterward. Caesar exiled Arsinoe to Ephesus; it would fall to Cleopatra's next Roman lover, Mark Antony, to dispose of the sibling at Cleopatra's direction.

Cleopatra's other younger brother, also Ptolemy (XIV), was appointed to share the throne with her but the ruler was Cleopatra, and Cleopatra was treated as the pharaoh by the Egyptians.

Cleopatra's Life Changes

In 46 BCE, the Egyptian royal family visited Rome; Cleopatra stayed in one of Caesar's villas. Caesar was married to Calpurnia Pisonis, and the citizens were scandalized by the blatant affair which flouted the decorum that they must have expected of their beloved Caesar. Rome would in time become known for licentiousness among its nobility but in Caesar's time, this sort of behavior was not tolerated. Although Caesarion was not named Caesar's heir, he did acknowledge his son and Cleopatra as his consort. In 44 BCE, upon the brutal assassination of her lover, Cleopatra returned to Egypt. After the death of Ptolemy XIV, who, it's assumed, must have been poisoned by his sister, Cleopatra named her son Caesarion as co-ruler.

Caesar's assassination left Rome in upheaval. The civil war which engulfed Rome directly affected Egypt's queen. She supported Octavian and Mark Antony against the assassins Brutus and Cassius, even becoming directly involved in the fighting when she sailed from Alexandria to join the supporters of Caesar.

However, a storm damaged her fleet and she had to return to Egypt. Antony and Octavion defeated Brutus and Cassius at the Battle of Philippi and they divided the spoils: Octavian ruled the western regions, and Antony the eastern provinces, which included Egypt.

Antony ordered the Egyptian monarch to appear before him in 41 BCE on charges of having provided aid to Caesar's assassins. But Cleopatra was not about to do his bidding; she came in her own time and when she did arrive, she was dressed as the goddess of love and beauty, Aphrodite.

Mark Antony had a wife in Rome; he'd married up, wedding the sister of Octavian. But once again, Egypt's queen played homewrecker. Cleopatra became his lover and they would be a couple for ten years, with three children born to their union. He eventually divorced Octavia and married Cleopatra. A year after spending the winter with Mark Antony in Alexandria, Cleopatra gave birth to Alexander Helios and Cleopatra Selene II, twins.

In 36 BCE, Antony fathered another child named Ptolemy Philadelphus. Cleopatra's children profited from Antony's military conquests; Alexander Helios was crowned ruler of Armenia, Media, and Parthia, and daughter Cleopatra Selene II was made queen of Cyrenaica and Libya; Ptolemy Philadelphus also had a coronation making him the ruler of Phoenicia, Syria, and Cilicia. But the declaration that Caesarion was the true heir to Julius Caesar was a threat to Octavian, who had been named Caesar's heir in his uncle's will.

Watching from Rome, Octavian decided that his partner in the Triumvirate was an enemy, and went to war against Egypt in 31 BCE. Defeated at the Battle of Actium the following year, Antony and Cleopatra recognized that defeat was final and fatal. But neither was willing to allow Octavian, who invaded Egypt, to execute them.

Antony died first; believing that Cleopatra had already omitted suicide, he stabbed himself with his sword. However, when he learned that she still lived, he was brought to Cleopatra, who was in hiding, to die in her arms. Captured by Octavian, and informed of her fate in no uncertain terms, Cleopatra was determined to die, and made several attempts before the one that ultimately succeeded. The legend which has prevailed, and which seems credible, is that Cleopatra died from an asp bite. There were theories that she was killed by Octavian, and also that she was poisoned. When Octavian had his triumphant march to Rome to celebrate his victory, he didn't have the Egyptian queen in chains as would have been her fate had she been alive; instead, she was there in effigy, with an asp clinging to her image.

Octavian murdered Caesarion; her children by Mark Antony were paraded in Rome as part of Octavian's victorious processional through the city that now belonged to him alone. Octavian then gave the children to his sister, Mark Antony's former wife, to raise.

Why Cleopatra Matters
Cleopatra VII Philopator wasn't all romance. She's credited with introducing Caesar to Sosigenes of Alexandria, the astronomer who first devised leap days and leap years for the calendar. It's difficult to envision

the two lovers sharing pillow talk about calendars, but Caesar did revise the calendar that was in use at the time.

Lost in the legend of Cleopatra is the woman who made what was actually a wise political choice when she got Rome to intervene on her behalf in Egypt's affairs; it was beyond the point where she could seek complete independence for her nation, so she chose the next best option: powerful leaders who recognized her as pharaoh. She was a popular ruler among her people—the name Philopator means lover of her country—and the fact that she bothered to learn the native language when other rulers would have restricted themselves to Greek indicates that she took her role seriously.

Plutarch wrote that it was not her beauty that captivated, but the charm of her presence. "There was an attraction in her person and in her conversation that, along with a peculiar force of character in her every word and action, laid all who associated with her under her sell." That was certainly the case with Julius Caesar and Mark Antony.

As the mother of Caesar's child, it's understandable that she regarded her son, and not Caesar's nephew Octavian, as the heir, although it's not surprising that Octavian did not share this view.

It's a matter of significance that the last pharaoh of Egypt was a queen in a time when kings predominated. She ruled over her nation, and her appeal to two of the most powerful men of the times does not diminish her. They fell in love with Cleopatra, and while her affections were genuine, she also used their power to benefit her position on the throne and the status of her country. That she lost her realm was not because of her sex; the Romans were just as successful in overcoming male rulers on their march to empire. That she maintained her own identity when those long-lost kings are nameless says much about the woman who was Cleopatra.

Isabella the Catholic 1451-1504

Who was Isabella?

To be third in the line to the Castilian throne of Spain in the 15th century, a time when disease and mortality ruled with as much power as any reigning monarch, meant that one had a very good chance of reaching the throne in due time. But for a woman in that position to become the reigning sovereign seemed less plausible. Nonetheless, Isabella of Castile, born in 1451, was in line to rule the throne after her half-brother Henry and younger brother Alfonso. By the time she was 23, she had become the Queen of Castile, had married Ferdinand of Aragon and united the two Spanish kingdoms, and given every indication that she would be a royal force with which to be reckoned.

During her reign, she brought order and prosperity to a country that had been lawless and financially impoverished under her brother's rule, introduced financial stability to the country and established a legal standard for coinage, administered a less unwieldy household, sought professional administrators rather than entitled nobles to serve on the Royal Council, thus minimizing the influence the nobles had in government, established a form of personal justice when she and the King would allow their subjects to approach them with complaints, created a comprehensive body of law to replace the cumbersome legal code, defeated Grenada, sponsored the journeys of Christopher Columbus, introduced the Spanish Inquisition to the country whose purpose was to rout out heretics—which was anyone who wasn't Roman Catholic—and force them to convert or leave the country, arranged political marriages for her offspring, received the title of Catholic Monarch from Pope Alexander VI, achieved the physical unification of Spain, and gave birth to five living children from seven pregnancies.

To understand who she was and what she accomplished, it's imperative to understand the world in which she lived. In a world where religion was a matter of national security, it's impossible to take Isabella out of her times; her belief in God sustained her through tragedy and trial, her commitment to Catholicism meant that other faiths were heresy, and heresy undermined the government. Perhaps heightening her piety was her confessor, Tomas de Torquemada, who would later become infamous for his zeal in implementing the Spanish Inquisition. To evaluate her through a modern prism is to take away the political reflexes of her era. Modern students may cringe at her religious authoritarianism, but in a period of time when monarchs ruled by divine right, the Queen was answerable only to God.

In the Beginning

Europe was a continent of competing dynasties united by marriage and divided by tempting boundaries and ceaseless ambitions. Isabella's mother was from the royal house of Portugal; her father was the king of Castile and Leon. After the death of King John brought her older half-brother Henry IV to the throne of Castile, Isabella and her younger brother Alfonso were raised in their widowed mother's household until the King brought them to his court; he feared that the ruthless nobles would use his siblings' claim to the throne as a ploy to overthrow him and gain power. He had reason for his fears; the nobles possessed great power, and Henry was not a commanding monarch.

In fact, Henry was an incompetent king under whose rule the nation became rife with lawlessness; he was a spendthrift whose extravagant ways crippled the Castilian economy; and he was childless except for a daughter whose paternity was in doubt. Henry's wife, the sister of the king of Portugal, was neither faithful nor discreet. A power struggle ended when Alfonso, age 14, died, whether of poisoning or the plague is unknown, and Isabella, showing a political astuteness beyond her young years, refused to accept the crown that the nobles offered to her. In response, her half-brother named her as heir to the throne.

She had been betrothed as a child to Ferdinand, the heir to the neighboring kingdom of Aragon, but in order to marry him, she had to first obtain a dispensation from the future Pope Alexander VI, more familiarly known as Rodrigo Borgia, because she and Ferdinand were second cousins. Her brother did not sanction their union, so Isabella opted to sneak away from court and Ferdinand had to travel in disguise in order for the marriage to take place. In retaliation, Henry named his daughter Juana (she of the disputed parentage) as his heir, but when Henry died, war erupted. Ultimately, Isabella ended up as Castile's queen and Juana ended up in a convent. But Juana was convinced of the legitimacy of her claim to the throne; when she sent letters, she defied Isabella's order, signing them "I, the queen."

The two kingdoms of Spain were united by the two monarchs, who ruled with complete authority in both realms. Fortunately, the two were also united in their views on what was needed to make Spain strong. Recognizing the overreaching ambitions of the nobility, one of the couple's first acts was to expand the power of the monarchy at the expense of the nobles. Isabella had learned a great deal during her royal apprenticeship and she was not going to give the nobles the same power they had used against her half-brother.

Early Influences

The most powerful influence in Isabella's life was her religious faith. She was committed to Roman Catholicism, known for her piety, and spent hours on her knees in prayer. There was no such thing, in those days, as a secular kingdom. It was God's will that Isabella ruled as Queen; therefore, her duty was to maintain a faithful kingdom. Her faith in God sustained her through the uncertainty of her early years, when Spanish nobles would have used her as a pawn against her brother the king, but even when she was a monarch in her own right, her religion gave her the fortitude that governed her actions. When she was a teenager, her brother decided to marry her off to an ally. Isabella took refuge in prayer. The praying worked; the intended bridegroom suddenly fell ill and died en route to meet his future bride. Faced with such an opportune result, who could blame her for relying on God, when humans had proven so unreliable?

She needed faith in God because her upbringing had provided little security. After the death of her father, she, her younger brother and mother lived in genteel poverty until her half-brother King Henry IV made her a member of the Queen's household. Her mother had gone into depression after childbirth and the condition became worse as time went on. Eventually, she could not remember the names of the people in her life, and no longer knew who she was. Mother and daughter were not close, and the relationship was not an affectionate one. In many ways, Isabella grew up with no one to rely on but herself. And her God.

Isabella's Life Changes

It could be said that Isabella's life changed at the age of six when she was betrothed to Ferdinand of Aragon. Her brother and Ferdinand's father intended to unite the two Spanish kingdoms but there was little security in the marriage market. There were other offers of matrimony, but the steadfast princess did not waver from that childhood engagement, showing that her resolve was not easily shaken. At the age of 18, she negotiated, on her own, with the King of Aragon to marry his son. Because the two were related, the pope's permission was sought in order to receive a dispensation. Ferdinand was a year younger when they united their crowns and countries in marriage. Approximately one million people lived in Aragon; Castile was three times as large as Aragon, with a population ranging from six to seven million.

While historians mark their marriage as the point at which Spain effectively became one country, the truth is that Castile and Aragon retained separate identities. One of the reasons for this is because neither kingdom became their home. Their court was a mobile one, in large part because the youthful monarchs were challenged by issues which had plagued previous rulers, particularly to maintain support from the local feudal lords.

How to implement royal dominance when it had been lacking? The monarchs created the Holy Brotherhood, a judicial force which was designed to not only act as a military peacekeeping unit, but also to reinforce royal authority against the nobility. With troops and courts, the Holy Brotherhood was empowered to deal with criminals from arrest to trial. They were so successful in restoring order to the Castilians that the Brotherhood was abolished in 1498.

From the 12th century, temporary organizations had been formed to maintain internal peace and protect against local criminals as well as nobilities who made and obeyed their own laws.

Showing shrewdness in advance of their years, Ferdinand and Isabella centralized this security force, giving them a considerable amount of jurisdiction. They were not known for clemency.

Further establishment of a uniform judicial system came with the creation of the Royal Council, with magistrates appointed to rule the villages and cities. This innovation played an integral role in the evolution of Spain as one of the first powerful nation-states of Europe.

In some ways, Isabella showed a very modern awareness of the trappings of monarchy. She and Ferdinand employed the symbol of the yoke so that the illiterate in Spain would recognize the royal crest of the joined kingdoms. The yoke was tied with the Gordian knot, arrows, and the initials of the king and queen. As monarchs of the two kingdoms, their unification of Spain did not include Granada, which was under the control of the Muslims. That however, would not last.

It's important to remember that in Isabella's day, religion was an ultimate arbiter in terms of loyalty and identify. The peninsula was home to a multicultural population that included Muslims and Jews as well as

Christians, something unusual in Europe during its medieval heritage.

The introduction of the Spanish Inquisition into Spain, viewed in those days as a security measure, meant that Spain was a Catholic-or-else country. Jews had the option of converting to Christianity, or they were required to leave Spain without their money, arms, or horses. But their conversion was viewed with suspicion and those who were accused of secretly following their original faith practices were arrested, imprisoned, tortured and sometimes burned at the stake. The Inquisition famously credited to the Spanish was a papal invention of the 12th century, one which Ferdinand and Isabella imported first to Castile in 1478 and later to the entire country of Spain. It's interesting to note that the Inquisition found a unique means of punishment to preserve its reputation for not shedding blood: when the death penalty was invoked, it was referred to as "relaxation" because the accused was relaxed to the state, which fulfilled the sentence.

For Christian rulers, service to the Prince of Peace was best accomplished by making war on those who held different beliefs. In 1482, the Granada War got underway with the support of the pope who levied a tithe and a crusade tax to invest in the battle. The war went on for 10 years. In 1492, the army of Ferdinand and Isabella defeated the Muslim forces at Granada. At first, the Muslims were allowed to keep their property, be ruled by their own laws, customs, and religion. But when the archbishop of Toledo ordered a policy of forced conversion, unrest was the result. In 1493, Muslims were given the choice of expulsion from Spain, now completely united under Catholic rule, or conversion   to   Christianity.

The year 1492 was a momentous one for Isabella the Catholic and her husband. It was the year when the Jewish ghettos were created, forcing them to live in segregation from the Christians. Taxation followed. Finally, the Jews were given four months to become Catholics or leave Spain. Thousands of Jews left Spain for Portugal, Italy, the Low Countries, North Africa and the regions of the Ottoman Empire.

The man known as Admiral of the Ocean Sea was searching for the Indies. Instead, he discovered the

Bahamas, Cuba, Santo Domingo, Puerto Rico, Trinidad, and the coast of Venezuela. Thanks to the wealth that returned to Spain from the New World, the kingdom of Ferdinand and Isabella became the dominant power in Europe from the end of the 16th century until the middle of the 17th century.

In 150, Isabella died, age 53. She had ordered that she was to be buried in the robes of a Franciscan, in order to usher her into heaven. Her role in bringing the Inquisition to Spain, seen as proof of her faith in her era, is regarded in modern times as evidence of the extreme religious prejudice which created so much torment for so many.

Why Isabella Matters

Isabella is known as the monarch who financed the voyages of Christopher Columbus to the New World, bringing treasure, prestige, and new boundaries back to the Spanish Empire. What people may not know is that, had her wishes been heeded, the native peoples of the new lands would have had a very different fate because the Queen was opposed to enslavement of the natives; she regarded them as her subjects.

The effects of the Inquisition ultimately served to stifle Spanish intellectual pursuits, as libraries were under the control of the Inquisition and thousands of books were burned. But it's interesting that the Spanish arts flourished at the same time as the Inquisition held power, with artist El Greco and writers Lope de Vega and Miguel Cervantes, whose *Don Quixote* is regarded as the first modern European novel.

Isabella's sphere of influence would have been remarkable for any leader governing today: for a woman of the Renaissance era to undertake the work she did was entirely remarkable.

To honor the Queen for her achievements, the Order of Isabella the Catholic was created four hundred years after her death, with the intention of rewarding Spaniards and foreigners who had demonstrated allegiance to Spain. On the 400th anniversary of Columbus' voyage to the new world, the United States issued a postage stamp depicting the Queen and her explorer, the first woman honored on an American stamp.

In the beginning years of Spain under the rule of Ferdinand and Isabella, the country was a poor one. But as the rulers solidified their power and expanded their sphere of influence, the poor country became an empire. The unification of Spain laid the groundwork for a nation that would use its wealth and its religious zeal in a manner which required the other nations of Europe to pay heed.

Her influence in Europe extended beyond her death thanks to the political marriages she arranged for her offspring. Two of her children married into the Portuguese royal family and established a strong alliance which nurtured peace. Her second daughter married the son of the Holy Roman Emperor, a marriage which supported a power structure that enhanced Spanish security. Isabella's grandson, Charles, who inherited a united Spain and was a power player in European politics, also inherited the title of Holy Roman Emperor. Beyond the Iberian Peninsula, marriage between Isabella's son John and a member of the Hapsburg dynasty united Spain with Austria. Daughter Catherine of Aragon was married to Henry VIII, and when Henry, eager for a son and a divorce, sought to have Aunt Catherine removed from her royal

English title, Charles, who had sacked Rome and had the Pope at his mercy, was standing in the way. The Tudor divorce was at an impasse and the dynasty was imperiled. What could a king do? If the king was Henry VIII, the answer was inevitable.

Henry took matters into his own hands; he cast off his Spanish queen and cast off Rome, turned England into a Protestant nation and married Anne Boleyn, who would, in short order, give birth to the future Elizabeth I before losing her head just as Isabella's daughter lost her crown. Unwittingly, Isabella the devout Catholic, through her knack for making dynastic marriages, raised a daughter who was steadfast in her own faith and refused the King's wishes, turning England into what Isabella would have regarded as a nation of heretics.

Mary Wollstonecraft the Feminist 1759-1797

Who was Mary Wollstonecraft?

Mary Wollstonecraft Godwin died before she was 40, but during those few years, she was an author, wife, and mother, a woman who made a name for herself when females were not encouraged to call attention to their achievements. She might have remained another of the forgotten females of the world of arts and letter if not for several episodes in her life which would establish her as a pioneering woman who was born in the wrong time. She defied convention, had love affairs while unmarried and gave birth to a daughter out of wedlock, then married philosopher William Godwin and died ten days after delivering the daughter who would go on to write the classic horror novel *Frankenstein* and live her own unconventional life with poet Percy Bysshe Shelley.

But with the rise of feminism and the women's suffrage movement in the early 1900s, Mary Wollstonecraft's contributions were re-examined, and

her best known work, *A Vindication of the Rights of Women*, became one of the foundations of the budding feminist movement. Had she been born today, she would have been a fixture on the talk show circuit, sharing her views as a media icon, and had countless followers on social media. But when she was born, women were a long way away from finding a welcoming audience if they dared to take center stage.

In the Beginning

Mary Wollstonecraft may have come to her feminist principles early, thanks to a bullying father who failed to provide for his seven children, beat his wife, drank to excess, and wrested control of Mary's inheritance from her. She was keenly aware of the favoritism shown to her brother, seeing the evidence that men were valued vastly more than women. Mary was protective of her mother and sisters, and when her father was violent, she would lie outside her mother's bedroom so that her father could not do her harm. Her father, after abandoning his trade as a weaver, traveled with his family across England and Wales in a futile attempt to become a gentleman farmer.

Early Influences

Mary was not to find harmony within her family. But she received solace in her friendship with the family of her friend Jane Arden, whose intellectual interests provided a means for the young woman to share her love of reading. Because the father dabbled in science and philosophy, Mary was able to enjoy the benefits of a social circle that encouraged learning and thinking. Another friendship, this one with a young woman named Fanny Blood, would be a powerful one and Mary credited Fanny as the woman who inspired her freedom of thought.

The two girls made plans to provide emotional and financial support for each other, but the immediacy of Mary's domestic situation sent her to seek employment. She became a companion to a Bath widow in 1787.

In 1780 she returned home to nurse her dying mother. Early on, Mary showed her independence and disregard for conformity when she encouraged her sister to leave not only her husband, but also the child to whom she had just given birth. That the result was her sister's ostracism from society and inability to provide for herself was a by-product of rebellion which Mary did not foresee. Throughout her life, she would act according to her emotions and was not governed by restraint, even when prudence might have proven the easier course of action. She and her sister started a school in a progressive community where ideas about equality were not viewed with suspicion. But in 1785, she left the school to nurse her friend Fanny, who was dying from consumption and died the next year. After Fanny's death, Wollstonecraft went to Ireland as the governess to the daughters of Lord and Lady Kingsborough, although she had written that she would not like being a governess who would, because of her role, be shut out of society and debarred from friendship.

Lady Kingsborough seemed the embodiment of all that Wollstonecraft would despise when she wrote about the role of women and their exaggerated weakness, flirtatiousness, and dependence upon men for their own identify. The two did not get along and in 1787, the governess was dismissed.

Mary's Life Changes

In 1787 at the age of 28, she ventured into a new career as a writer, even though the prospects were limited. Financial independence, which she espoused in her writing, was something she achieved. She found a place to live in London and went to work; she reviewed books, taught herself French and German and translated writings in those languages. She was taken on as an editorial assistant and writer by a London publisher with radical philosophies. She wrote her first book, *Thoughts on the Education of Daughters*, and a biographical novel, *Mary, a Fiction*. She became part of a circle of intellectuals which included scientist Joseph Priestly, who promoted reason and reform over religion. These connections made her recognize that, for women, the lack of education was an insurmountable obstacle to financial security. Certainly she observed that many women showed no interest in education. They were more concerned with vanity and frivolity. But she blamed this shallowness on the lack of education which would have broadened their ability to discern.

A later generation would indict the bra as evidence of the oppression of clothing upon women.

Wollstonecraft blamed corsets for preventing women from having similar opportunities for physical activity. Males were encouraged to engage in outside activities; women were steered toward inside pursuits such as sewing. She wrote, "Taught from their infancy that beauty is woman's scepter, the mind shapes itself to the body, and, roaming round its gilt cage, only seeks to adorn its prison." Because, she believed, the mind and the body were joined, women needed to become physically stronger if they were going to break free of the oppression that a male-dominated society used to subjugate them.

She also became part of London's intellectual scene, and met the man who would eventually become her husband, the philosopher William Godwin. However, at their first meeting, there was no indication that they would one day marry. Mary became involved with a married man, Henry Fuseli, an artist, who eventually rejected her. Their affair ended when she suggested that she, Fuseli, and Fuseli's wife adopt a ménage-a-trois living arrangement.

From failed romance to the French revolution, Mary

traveled to France to forget her broken heart and sample the fervor that was roiling France, becoming part of the British expatriate community in Paris. She wrote *Reflections on the Revolution in France* and found herself mentioned in the same breath as Joseph Priestly and Thomas Paine for her writings and radical views. Wollstonecraft was not afraid to take on intellectual heavyweights such as Jean-Jacques Rousseau in her defense of women's rights to education. She deplored the traditional marital role of females as obedient, lovely inferiors to their husbands. Her comment, "To marry for a support is legal prostitution," was bold and insightful in a society where marriage was a woman's only means of social achievement.

The violence of the French Revolution was just as jarring as its endorsement of equality, as people began to seriously question the role of the monarchy. Taking the concepts of revolution to her own gender, she wrote *A Vindication of the Rights of Women* in 1792, which held that women were human beings first, equal to men, and not a different species to men. Paris in the throes of Revolution must have been an inspiration to the ardent Mary, who was a witness as traditional conventions were cut away from French society as swiftly as the guillotine would decapitate the heads of the aristocrats. She observed that the sympathy which Edmund Burke expressed for the guillotined female aristocrats failed to include the distress of the poverty-stricken mothers trying to raise and feed their children. Despite her support of the intellectual aims of the French Revolution, she was disillusioned by the bloodthirsty executions of the Jacobin movement. Her book, *Historical and Moral View Of The Origin and Progress of The French Revolution*, written in 1794, represented her effort to support her belief in equality with the destructiveness of the war.

Wollstonecraft's nontraditional lifestyle exhibited a personal form of chaos. Once again, she fell in love with a married man, an American named Gilbert Imlay and gave birth to a daughter Fanny, named after Fanny Blood, who had died of failing health. When the British declared war on France and Mary's British citizenship would have endangered her, his American identity concealed her nationality even though they were not married. Paris was erupting in violence all around her; King Louis had already been guillotined. Then in the midst of the bloodthirsty chaos, Imlay vanished and

Mary discovered that her lover had abandoned her to fend for herself in a dangerous and hostile country.

She was, of course, heartbroken and devastated. But she was a writer. This passionate woman attempted to win him back by means more prosaic than romantic. She wrote another book, this one based on travels she took in an effort to help him recoup his finances. But the broken romance led to a second suicide attempt. The first failed attempt had been by taking laudanum but Imlay had rescued her. The second attempt was to be by drowning, but she was spotted in the water, and she was saved from death again.

She rebounded from her emotional loss. Her literary life resuming, she became part of the circle of writers again, and this time, she and William Godwin were not so disappointed in each other. For Godwin, reading the book she had written about Imlay, *Letters Written in Sweden, Norway and Denmark*, her account of her failed romance, inspired him to fall in love with her and he praised her genius. He wrote that "If ever there was a book calculated to make a man in love with its author, this appears to me to be the book." Goodwin was the antithesis of the traditional husband; he saluted his wife's courage and originality.

Godwin had previously voiced his opposition to marriage in his writing; Mary had not been married to the father of her child. Both stances brought controversy into their lives when they decided to wed in 1797 so that their unborn child would be legitimate. During her pregnancy, she was working on what would be her last book, *The Wrongs of Woman; or Maria*. The novel's heroines are both living outside of society's accepted rules; one character is a prostitute, the other an adulteress.

Their marriage was somewhat unconventional—they lived in two adjoining houses, often communicating by letter—but happy. It was also brief. Mary died of septicemia or childbed fever, a frequent cause of death for women in the 18th century, the same year as she was married. Her tombstone paid tribute to her most famous writing: Mary Wollstonecraft Godwin, Author of *A Vindication of the Rights of Women*. Godwin published the *Posthumous Works of Mary Wollstonecraft* and his *Memoirs of the Author of a*

Vindication of the Rights of Women.

Godwin made a serious mistake when he published such a candid memoir of his wife after her death. What were to him indications of Mary's courage and spirit were shocking revelations to an audience that did not expect a husband to disclose his wife's premarital love affairs, suicide attempts, and illegitimate child. Mary's reputation was in tatters and would remain so for a century after her death.

Why Mary Wollstonecraft Matters

But Mary's literary bequests proved more powerful than the scandal. Her book was read by poet Elizabeth Barrett Browning, whose poem *Aurora Leigh* supported Wollstonecraft's views on education for women. Activist Lucretia Coffin Mott, who helped to coordinate the Seneca Falls Convention in the United States in 1848 in support of women's rights, also read Wollstonecraft's work. British author George Eliot, the alias of Mary Ann Evans who wrote under a male name so that she would be taken seriously as a writer, shared her thoughts on the legitimacy of Wollstonecraft's stance on women and education.

For the 21st century, feminism and women's rights are regarded as mainstream social practice in many parts of the world. But in the era in which Wollstonecraft lived, loved, and wrote, her belief in the individual rights of women against the established power elite ruled by men, was both absurd and shocking.

Writing in the 20th century, Virginia Woolf described Wollstonecraft's success over her early death. "She is alive and active, she argues and experiments, we hear her voice and trace her influence even now among the living." As the move for women's rights strengthened, Wollstonecraft's tainted reputation underwent a renovation. More women who would become renowned in fields as varied as literature and the reform movement studied her life. From being a casualty of a constrained and narrow society that could not fathom a woman occupying status equal to a man, she became a standard bearer for a future generation.

Juana Azurduy 1781-1862

Simon Bolivar, born 1783

Pancho Villa, born 1878

Fidel Castro, born 1926

Che Guevara, born 1928

Jose Marti, born 1853

Emiliano Zapata, born 1879

This list of Latin American revolutionaries and freedom fighters demonstrates that the countries which once suffered under Spanish rule did not lack for heroes committed to fighting for freedom from oppression. But it also points out that when the freedom fighter is a woman, even a detail as significant as the year she was born may be lost in obscurity.

Juana Azurduy Bermudez was born in either 1780 or

1781, but if the exact year of her birth is not known, time made up for it by giving her a long life that did not end until 1862. Although she died in poverty, her contributions to the cause of freedom in colonial South America, once almost forgotten, have been re-evaluated as history moved into deeper and broader paths where the influence of women has undergone re-assessment.

In the Beginning

Born in the town of Chuquisaca, Viceroyalty of the Rio de la Plata in what is now Sucre, Bolivia to a wealthy, property-owning father, Don Matias Azurduy and his indigenous wife, Doña Eulalia Bermudez, Juana Azurduy Bermudez was a mestizo, half-Spanish, half-indigenous. Unions between the Spanish men and the native women were common because Spanish women had tended to remain in Spain rather than move to the New World. The girl who would grow up to challenge Spanish authority may have received her indoctrination into the unjust practices of the existing legal system early in her life. When her father was killed by Spaniards, the killer was not prosecuted for his crime.

Azurduy's entrance into the Santa Theresa Convent at the age of 12 was short-lived. The spirited young girl was expelled from the convent for her rebellious ways which were clearly contrary to the rule of obedience in a religious order. In other parts of the world, they would have been just as contrary, but in her country, with anger against the autocratic Spanish seething, and the drive for freedom growing stronger, Azurduy's disinclination to follow convention suited the times. In her early twenties (again, the dates are not specific) she married Manuel Ascencio Padilla, who shared her commitment to the cause of freedom.

Padilla was the son of a landowner in what was then Peru and is now Bolivia who joined the army when he was young. He was studying the law when he made the decision to halt his education to marry Juana Azurduy in 1805.

Early Influences

The western hemisphere was, in the age of exploration, easy prey for the Europeans who crossed the ocean searching for gold, conquest, and whatever profit could be obtained, whether it was precious metals or converted souls, from the New World. Latin America became the colony of the Spanish Empire; the conquistadors conquered the mighty Aztecs and Mayans, enslaved a population, and brought lethal diseases for which the native population had no immunity. But several centuries later, Europe would unwittingly send a new export across the ocean, something which was, in its way, just as potent.

In the early 19th century, the Napoleonic Wars had become a global outbreak of battles with collateral effects which reached across the Atlantic Ocean; the invasion of Spain by Napoleon sent ripples of alarm into the colonies that Spain ruled. South America was already inflamed with the native peoples seeking independence from the Spanish who had dominated the continent since the era of exploration and conquest several hundred years before. A slave uprising in 1791 against the French on the colony of Dominque led to the creation of Haiti. Revolts in Brazil and Venezuela followed. By the year 1820, the Spanish made up only 10 percent of the armies that supported the regions' royalist regimes, and there were only

10,001 Spanish soldiers remaining in the Americas.

Simon Bolívar, a Venezuelan leader who had been born into wealth, had spent time in Europe and when he returned home, he brought the radical ideas of the Enlightenment with him. The ideals of social reform were powerful and popular for the people who had been dominated by European rule for so long. Bolivar's army invaded Venezuela in 1813, fighting under the slogan "War to the death." The royalists won more than the rebels, but Bolivar's determination would eventually prove victorious. Not easily, however; it would take time, and much loss of life, before independence drove the royalists from power.

There is no way of knowing for certain how much Juana knew of the dramatic events that were transforming the world, but she was well aware of one thing. She knew that life for the native-born people of her homeland was unfair and oppressive, and the girl who had stirred up rebellion in the convent was now a woman ready to fight against what she opposed.

Juana's Life Changes

Argentina's war for independence began in 1810. In 1809, unrest in the country led to the overthrow of the Spanish Vice Regency and the beginning of insurrections by guerilla fighters. One of those guerillas was Juana Azurduy, who joined Manuel Belgrano's army in 1810; as a token of his esteem for her bravery, Belgrano gifted her with a saber, obviously taking seriously her zeal and willingness to fight. He also esteemed her husband, who was the civil and military commander of an area known as the Republic of La Laguna, fighting with 2,000 Indian guerillas. Belgrano, along with Juan Jose Castelli and Jose de San Martin, was fighting the royalist forces who owed their loyalty to Spain. Belgrano seemed an unlikely revolutionary, with his background as a Buenos Aires economist, lawyer and politician. He, like Bolivar, had returned home from his education in Europe inflamed with the ideals of the Enlightenment. When he was elected to the viceroyalty of the Rio de la Plata, he made the attempt to promote the reforms that he had absorbed, but those ideas were rejected. He then began to work in support of autonomy from the Spanish regime. That support would eventually take a military turn.

When Juana's hometown was retaken by Spanish forces in 1811, the family's land was confiscated. Juana and her four children were captured, and then rescued by her husband. The children were as much a part of the struggle for freedom as their parents, and the results would not always be happy ones. Juana and her husband, whose equal dedication to the cause of freedom was a cornerstone of their marriage, raised a battalion to fight the Spanish; she is estimated at one point to have commanded an army whose strength was approximately 6,000 troops.

Waiting for a counterattack from the royal forces after victory in battle, her husband marched to fight while Juana took refuge with the children. She learned that the Spanish were heading toward the Segura Valley, placing her husband was in danger. But she had perils of her own to face as the only adult in an unfamiliar mountain area with no food or shelter, and children depending on her. Two of her children died before Padilla could rescue them and the remaining two died of dehydration on the return to the Segura Valley. Of the five children of Juana and her husband, only the youngest one, a daughter, would survive the war for independence to which her parents had committed themselves.

Freedom fighters expect to sacrifice for the cause that consumes them, but Juana paid a high price for her contribution to the cause of freedom. Perhaps she was able to channel her grief into the rousing physical exertions of war. She was fearless in battle, earning a promotion to lieutenant colonel in 1816 after she led a cavalry charge that brought the capture of the Spanish standard during fighting in the Cerror Rico of Potosi, the primary location of the much-needed silver upon which Spain depended.

But in November of the same year, when she was pregnant, her husband was killed in battle trying to save her after she was injured. In order to recover his body, Juana led a counterattack, but the battle itself was lost and she and some of her army escaped to northern Argentina where she continued to fight. After her appointment as commander of the Northern army of the Revolutionary Government of the United Provinces of the Rio de la Plata, she established an insurrection zone, forcing the Spanish to withdraw. In a military episode which no male soldier could hope to duplicate, Juana was fighting in battle under the command of Argentinian Martin Güemes when she had to pause to give birth to her daughter Luisa. After the baby was delivered, she returned to the fight.

Güemes died, and Juana, her military career finished, herself left impoverished with a daughter to raise, moved to Sucre. When Bolivia became independent in 1825, Juana asked for her property to be returned to her, but her request was ignored. She would not be the only military leader of the independence movement to die in poverty. Manuel Belgrano had lost his wealth to the cause of war, and when he was on his deathbed, he could only pay his doctor with some of the few possessions that remained to him.

But they had been successful in their battles for their countries. Juana's life was changed after she returned to civilian life, and the sacrifices that she had made in the war for independence cost her not only her husband, but four of her children. But she fought the fight for freedom using guerilla-style tactics to contest the grip of Spanish authority. She died in 1862, poor and forgotten, but as history began to realize that women had done more than sit on the sidelines while the fight for independence was waged, Juana's contributions were also re-discovered.

Why Juana Azurduy Matters

One hundred years after Juana Azurduy's death, her remains were exhumed and brought to the city of Sucre, her birthplace. With the restoration of her fame comes its trappings and the woman who lost her land has become a landmark.

In 2014, as part of an outdoor exhibition of famous Latin Americans, a sculpture of her was displayed on the grounds of Washington D.C.'s Pan American Union Building. In 2009, she was posthumously awarded the rank of general in Argentina's military. Argentina's *The National Programme for Women's Rights and Participation* is named in her honor. Flights into Sucre, Bolivia, arrive at the Juana Azurduy Padilla International Airport, named for the woman who gave so much in the fight for independence against Spain. Azurduy Province, officially the Provincia de Juana Azurduy de Padilla, was named in her honor. She is also perhaps unique in becoming a teaching tool as the subject of a cartoon created to teach children about Argentina's history.

Bolivian President Evo Morales commissioned a statue of Azurduy to replace a statue of Christopher Columbus. The sculptor worked with 45 assistants on the statue. In July, 2015, a statue of Azurduy was unveiled in Buenos Aires, Argentina by the presidents of both countries. At a height of 52 feet, weighing 25 tons, the statue was heralded as the tallest in Argentina. Some Argentinians of Italian descent, as well as the mayor of Buenos Aires, protested the removal of the statue of Columbus, but Argentina's President Cristina Fernandez de Kirschner defended the removal of the Columbus statue in favor of a statue of a woman who fought for independence in South America.

The statue was further evidence of Azurduy's significance as a symbol of "Patri Grande" or Big Homeland, which refers to the integration process taking place in the region. The statue also served as a commemoration of the bonds between Argentina and Bolivia and the history that the countries share. They share the legend of one of history's true freedom fighters, a woman who dedicated her life to the cause of independence and sacrificed much to achieve it.

Rescued from lost history, Juana Azurduy has finally been found.

Victoria the Queen 1819-1901

Who was Queen Victoria?

From the history of a woman about whom relatively few details are known, to that of a queen whose 63 years on the throne of England are meticulously catalogued, we see that not only were women acquiring more influence in the new century, but society was more diligent about recording the events of the their lives. Of course, it helps when the woman herself was an enthusiast diarist who wrote 2500 words each day.

The familiar portrait of the rotund queen staring imperiously into the camera leads subsequent generations to see her as a dowdy woman whose youth must have been decorous and orderly. Her reputation as an arbiter of rigid morality ignores the woman who frankly felt an exuberant and most nonVictorian passion for her husband Prince Albert. Strict in adhering to duty, disapproving of her rather indulgent and promiscuous son, Victoria was a much more complicated woman than her image indicates.

When she ascended to the throne in 1837, at the age of 18, she would be the royal face of Great Britain for more than six decades. Her reign encompassed the dramatic changes that the 19th century underwent, as carriages were replaced by automobiles, science transformed everyday life, and communication became more widespread. When Great Britain's achievements exceeded its national boundaries, the title of empress was added to her name.

In the Beginning

Alexandrina Victoria was eight months old when her father died. She was named for her godfather, Alexander I of Russia, and her mother, also Victoria. George IV had forbidden her from being named Charlotte, Elizabeth, or Georgina. She went by the nickname of Drina for most of her childhood.

Victoria's father was the fourth son of King George III and her mother was the sister of King Leopold of the Belgians. Because her surviving uncles had no legitimate heirs, she was heir to the throne and a member of a spectacularly dysfunctional family. Two of her uncles, one of whom was the future George IV, were estranged from their wives.

The young princess was sequestered from other people, and very much under her mother's thumb; Victoria even slept in her mother's bedroom. She mainly was in contact with her mother, the Duchess of Kent, and Sir John Conroy, rumored to be the Duchess of Kent's lover. They may have been able to control her interactions with others, but they could not control her destiny.

When her uncle became William IV, she was acknowledged as the heir and future queen; King William was so distrustful of Victoria's mother's dominating nature that he vowed to live long enough for Victoria to turn 18 so that the Duchess of Kent would not be a regent. He won his wish; when the sheltered princess was crowned, she was of an age to rule without her mother as regent. Writing of that momentous birthday, Victoria noted the crowds thronging the streets to show their affection. ". . . the anxiety of the people to see poor stupid me was very great, and I must say I am quite touched by it, and feel proud which I always have done of my country and of the English nation." In less than a month, Victoria would be the queen.

Early Influences

Lord Melbourne, the prime minister at the time of her accession to the British throne, became a favorite of the young queen as he steered her through the political waters of her constitutional role. Although she was the queen, the prime minister was as much a father figure as an advisor in her life. Her fondness for Melbourne meant that she was hostile to his successor, Sir Robert Peel. She would in the future be equally distant from William Gladstone, who she complained, spoke to her as if she were a public meeting instead of a woman.

Victoria's Uncle Leopold, the King of the Belgians, was the architect of the marriage between his niece, Victoria, and his nephew. Victoria was charmed by Albert's looks and charm, but she did not move to matrimony right away. The couple corresponded and visited, and in 1839, Victoria proposed marriage. She was, after all, the Queen, and she outranked him. In her diary, Victoria wrote that the day when she proposed marriage to Albert was "the happiest brightest moment in my life."

At the age of 21, she married Albert of Saxe-Coburg and Gotha, age 20, one of the seemingly endless members of German minor royalty. Like Victoria, Albert's early life was not one of family harmony; his father had divorced his mother for adultery when he was a young boy. Albert's mother was exiled from court in 1824, when he was five years old. The woman of scandal married her lover and probably never saw her children again. She died of cancer when Albert was 11 years old. It's ironic that the couple which came to represent pillars of domestic order both came from families which had known their share of upheaval. Albert was mature beyond his years, and because he was a man who needed to have a purpose, he served his wife well as an advisor. On a personal level, he served as a mediator between mother and daughter and helped to ease the hostility that festered between them.

He tried to persuade Victoria to act as a neutral force between the political parties instead of adopting a partisan stance. His interest in social issues like the problem of child labor became her interest as well. Within two months after their marriage, the Queen was pregnant. Victoria, who would give birth to five daughters and four sons over the course of 17 years, was enthusiastic about her marital relations, despite the image that Victorians have of being prudish, but she detested pregnancy. In 1853, she was at least able to obtain ease from the pain of childbirth when delivering her eighth child. She had argued for chloroform for earlier pregnancies, but in addition to the concern that the drug might do harm, there was also the lingering belief that pain during childbirth was the will of God, and the fate of women to endure. Victoria thought otherwise and was not shy about saying so.

The royal couple's nine children all survived to adulthood; his biographer credited Albert with having a beneficial effect on the running of the nursery. Early in their marriage, Albert had Victoria's governess, Baroness Lehzen, removed from her position overseeing the nursery; the Baroness left England.

Although Victoria has been regarded as a woman who disliked her role as a mother, her diaries reveal a very different parent. She was not a distant parent, believing instead that children should spend as much time as possible with their mother and father. Her ladies-in-waiting noted that her children occupied a significant role in her daily routine. Her affection for children was not restricted solely to her own offspring. When her godchild died as a baby, Victoria wrote: "I cannot say how it grieves me. Such a sad event makes one think of one's own little treasures and how they might be taken from one."

For as long as he was her husband, Victoria and Albert shared their roles as parents. In fact, they shared many responsibilities as the ultimate English power couple. Albert was not initially popular among the Queen's subjects. Parliament made him a British citizen and he was given the title of "His Royal Highness" but the governing body would not make him a British peer; the amount of his annuity was reduced to an amount lower than what previous prince consorts had been given. But Albert seemed to have had a strong sense of his own identity and his own purpose as the husband of the Queen. Albert recognized his obligations to the country of the woman he had married, and he pursued his support of science, trade, industry and the arts. Thanks to his dedication and organization skills, The Great Exhibition of 1851 brought visitors—including Charles Darwin and Charlotte Bronte—and profits to Great Britain, as it celebrated the nation's impressive industrial achievements. In 1857, Victoria granted him the title of Prince Consort.

The country came to recognized Albert's beneficial role in the royal family. His influence over his wife was powerful, but stable. He had a gift for finance and was able to increase the revenues from the Duchy of Cornwall, the traditional inheritance of the Prince of Wales. He managed the royal estates and designed Osborne House, a private residence on the Isle of Wight. The government knew that he had access to Victoria's papers, drafted her correspondence, and met with her ministers. He was, a member of the government admitted, the king for all intents and purposes. He was an important figure in the country but, despite the legend, it was not Albert who introduced the Christmas tree to Great Britain.

The marriage was a successful one but like any marriage, private or public, it was not without emotion. Victoria had a temper, so much so that Albert feared that she had inherited the alleged madness (later determined to be porphyria and not insanity) of her ancestor, George III. During the times when she was irate, Albert would communicate with her by slipping notes under her door. For her part, Victoria, although she valued Albert's assistance in her official role, sometimes resented the fact that her frequent pregnancies increased his power and influence in a royal role that she was reluctant to share.

Victoria's Life Changes

As the mother of nine children, it was no surprise that Queen Victoria was not always pleased with their exploits. Her eldest son, Edward Albert, known in the family as Bertie, had never possessed his parents' strict moral code, and when rumors came to Albert that Edward had become sexually involved with an actress, he made the journey to Cambridge to confront his son. Not long after he returned, he was diagnosed with typhoid fever and died December 14, 1861. However, contemporary historians have noted that Albert had been ill for two years prior to his death, leading to an indication that he may have been afflicted with abdominal cancer, renal failure, or Crohn's disease.

Victoria blamed her son for Albert's death, and for the rest of her life, wore black for mourning. In all the houses that she and Albert had shared, she gave the order that nothing was to change; the linens were changed daily and hot water was brought to the room each morning.   Isolated from the public, she was referred to as the Widow of Windsor. She did not neglect her royal duties, but spent her time at Windsor Castle, Osborne House, and Balmoral House, the Sottish estate that she had acquired with Albert in 1847, instead of Buckingham Palace. Meanwhile, the absence of the Queen encouraged the growth of movements toward republican thinking in a period of time when revolution and reform were igniting all over Europe. But when her uncle Leopold advised her that it was time to make an effort to assume public duties, she assented to his advice. In 1866, she attended the opening of Parliament for the first time since Albert died.

As a widowed mother, Victoria's children remained a primary concern. She had always been critical of her son and heir, known in the family as Bertie, whose

84

morals were decidedly different from the ones with which he had been raised. But even her beloved daughter Vicky aroused the royal condemnation when she, as well as her sister, Alice, decided to breastfeed their children. They tried to keep the news from Victoria, who thought that nursing one's infants was disgusting, but of course she found out, and was not complimentary.

Victoria had a knack for finding things out. She instructed the family doctor to let her know intimate details regarding her daughter-in-law Alix, married to the future Edward VII, including when she was menstruating. Victoria would not schedule court balls if they would conflict with Alix's cycle.

The woman of the utmost propriety nonetheless had tongues wagging later in life. Balmoral was always a favorite residence of the Queen, a place of pleasant memories because she and Albert had purchased it. John Brown was her husband's ghillie, an outdoor servant who was in attendance during hunting and fishing outings. Brown did not treat her with the humbleness of a servant. He was a rugged, rough-edged man but the Queen didn't seem to mind. He reprimanded her, ordered her, and she was perfectly accepting of his manner. She commissioned a portrait of him, and created two medals—the Faithful Servant Medal and the Devoted Servant Medal—in his honor. When gossip started because of his familiarity, the Queen dismissed it as ill-natured. Because Brown slept in an adjoining room, the rumors circulated that they were lovers. The life-sized statue that Victoria commissioned of Brown was moved to an inconspicuous location after her son, Prince Edward, became king.

The Queen was almost as devoted to Brown as she was to her beloved Albert. When the Queen died in 1901, the new king, Edward VII did his best to eradicate the memory of Brown by destroying the busts and photographs of the man.

Victoria kept a journal of the events of her life. It's from her own words that we know of her delight on her wedding night, of her grief when her daughter Alice died on the anniversary of Albert's death, and of her sense of loss as her daughters married and left for thrones in other countries. We know that when an assassination attempt, one of several that failed, was made against her, she wrote that the concern of the public made it worth being shot at.

She became an empress in 1876 when India was brought into the Empire. In 1887, Great Britain commemorated the 50th anniversary of her accession to the throne. In 1896, she became the longest reigning monarch in English, Scottish or British history, an occasion to be celebrated at her Diamond Jubilee.

When she died on January 22, 1901, mourners found that she had written specific instructions on how to conduct her funeral. She wore a white dress and her wedding veil from her marriage to her beloved Albert; in her coffin, as she had requested, were placed one of Albert's dressing gowns, a plaster cast of his hand, and jewelry. Also included were a photograph of Brown, a lock of his hair, and a ring that Brown had given to her. In a sense, Queen Victoria was taking it with her; not so much the trappings of monarchy, but the mementos that mattered. She was a Victorian, sentimental and materialistic, surrendering her mortal body to God, but on terms of her choosing.

Why Victoria Matters

Victoria was a constitutional monarch who held no genuine power. But as the mother of nine children who married into Europe's royal families, she was the matriarch of the continent with an influence that in many ways bypassed Parliament; one of her unofficial titles was "grandmother of Europe." She maintained a strong hold on her family and while they might be titled Kaiser, Czar, and Prince to their subjects, they were Willie, Nicky, and Bertie to their royal relative.

Thanks to Victoria's practice of writing at length in her journal, historians have 122 volumes detailing her life as queen, wife, and mother. Her writing reveals her to have been very much involved in the political events over which she had influence; she was honest and emotional. She was as much an autocrat as the political setting of Great Britain would allow her to be, with a keen sense of what it meant to be royal, but she was also very much a woman.

One of Victoria's most powerful and unfortunate legacies came from her DNA. Two of her daughters were carriers for hemophilia. Her great-grandson, Alexei of Russia, was afflicted with the disease, and while it was not hemophilia which brought down the Romanov dynasty and led to the rise of the Bolsheviks, the royal family's reliance on the monk Rasputin had made the deteriorating situation in Russia worse. The family was taken captive by the Bolsheviks and murdered in 1918.

The English line of the family enjoyed more tranquility. In contrast to her hedonistic uncles, Victoria embodied the middle-class values which came to be known as Victorian. While Victoria and Albert were derided by the worldly and sophisticated players in society, their sturdy values may have played a role in what has kept the British monarchy secure on their thrones. They maintain some of the mystique of royalty, but little of the entitlement; the contemporary royals seem willing to treat their blue-blooded pedigree as part of the requirements of the job as they christen ships, tour factories, visit schools, and speak out on items of concern to their public.

Victoria is responsible for a bridal tradition which continues to this day. When it was time for her wedding to Albert, she decided not to follow the tradition of wearing a brightly colored dress. Instead, she wore white. Instead of wearing a crown, she wore a wreath of orange blossoms in her hair. Brides who make that journal down the aisle probably have no idea that they're following in royal footsteps.

A lasting tribute to the queen for her subjects came in 1856, when the Victoria Cross was introduced as an award for bravery on the part of British and Commonwealth troops in battle.

Marie Curie the Mother of Modern Physics 1867-1934

Who was Marie Curie

Marie Curie was a woman of firsts in a new century that would find itself bidding farewell to the world that was undergoing dramatic changes. The first woman to win a Nobel Prize, Marie Curie was also the first person—and the only woman—to win the award twice, as well as the only person honored with the Nobel Prize twice in multiple sciences, in physics and chemistry. She was the first female professor at Paris' Sorbonne, a school that she attended as a student. She was the first woman in all of Europe to receive a PhD when, in 1903, she presented her dissertation.

In the Beginning

Although she eventually would become a naturalized citizen of France, Maria Sklodowska was born in 1867 in Warsaw, Poland, one of five children of Bronislawa Boguska, who was a teacher, a pianist, a singer, and a principal of a school for girls. and Wladyslaw Sklodowski, who was a professor of mathematics and physics. Her mother was Catholic and Maria was raised in the faith, but by the time she was 20, she had left the church. Maria was fortunate to have parents who believed that daughters should receive the same education as sons. The youngest child in the family, Maria showed signs of intellectual prowess when she graduated first in her high school class at the age of 15, winning a gold medal for her accomplishments. Her mother was not there to enjoy her youngest child's achievement, as she had died of tuberculosis when Maria was 10.

Her desire to attend university was stymied by the refusal of the University of Warsaw to admit women. So Maria attended underground classes that were held in secret so that she could continue her studies. Family finances were troubled because her father had made unwise investments that cost him his savings. Maria became a governess at the age of 17, in order to provide financial support so that her older sister, who would go on to become a gynecologist, could attend medical school in Paris. They had agreed that when Bronya finished school, she would help provide funding for Maria. Maria worked as a governess and tutor for five years and then it was her turn.

In Paris, now calling herself Marie so that she would blend in better at the Sorbonne, the young student sacrificed her health for her studies when she discovered that she was not up to the standards of the Sorbonne. She attended the lectures of instructors Paul Appel, Gabriel Lippmann, and Edmond Bouty. Instead of sharing a residence with her sister, she took an apartment near the school so that she would have more studying time. In order to afford her rent, her meals often consisted of just bread and butter and tea. She met well known physicists Jean Perrin, Charles Maurain, and Aime Cotton. Once again, she was first in her class. She received a master's degree in physics in 1893, and a year later, after she was awarded a scholarship, she received a degree in mathematics. She began working in Lippmann's research laboratory.

Early Influences
When she received a research grant to study steel's magnetic properties and chemical composition, she needed lab space. That led to a meeting with Pierre Curie, who had invented instruments to measure electricity and magnetic fields. He found space for her

where he worked. The proximity worked in their favor, and they were married in 1895. They were married in a civil ceremony because Pierre did not have a religious affiliation and Marie no longer practiced her mother's Catholicism. Daughter Irene was born in 1897, but research and motherhood did not bring Marie's career to a halt, as she took a position teaching physics at a girls' school.

Marie's Life Changes

Using the instruments that her husband had invented, Marie focused her research on uranium rays. The term radioactive was coined by Marie to indicate materials that had the effect of emitting Becqueret rays, named after the French physicist Henry Becqueret. In order to test the theory, which intrigued her husband so much that he postponed his own work to share hers, the Curies needed more space. Marie worked late into the night in a shed they rented outside the school, separating the two ores, chalcolite and pitchblende, which they found were much more radioactive than just pure uranium.

She discovered radioactivity in thorium, and proved

that radioactivity is an atomic property and not a property of the interaction between elements. When she realized that the rays stayed constant regardless of the uranium's condition or form, because they came from the element's atomic structure, the field of atomic physics was born.

They published their findings in 1898, naming a new radioactive element called polonium which was named for Poland, Marie's native country. Soon after, they isolated a radioactive element that they named radium, from the Latin word for rays. In 1902, they extracted purified radium.

In 1903, Marie became Dr. Curie, the first European women to receive a doctorate in physics. The same year presented a conundrum for the Nobel Prize Committee; the members were reluctant to name a woman for the honor, but her husband credited his wife with the original research. The year 1903 was a banner year for her professionally, but also one of grief, as a baby that was born prematurely died. A second daughter, Eve, joined the family in 1904. Also in 1904, the Sorbonne's decision to give Pierre a professorship helped ease the financial constraints which the family faced. Marie's father-in-law joined the family so that he could care for his granddaughters while the parents pursued their work.

In 1906, however, grief returned to Marie, when Pierre was run over in a Paris street by a horse-drawn carriage and killed, leaving his wife a widow with two young daughters. She refused a national pension, but accepted the Sorbonne's offer of Pierre's chair; when she was elected a full professor two years later, she was the first woman to hold a chair at the Sorbonne. She had a philosophical response to tragedy. "Life is not easy for any of us. But what of that? We must have perseverance and above all confidence in ourselves. We must believe that we are gifted for something and that this thing must be attained."

But the Old Guard was reluctant to loosen the reins of dominance. By a single vote, she was refused election in the French Academy of Science because she was a woman. Marie didn't forget the insult, refusing to allow her name to be resubmitted for nomination, and denying the Academy the right to publish any of her research for a decade. Marie's second Nobel Prize came in 1911, after Pierre's death, for her discovery of polonium and radium.

But the Nobel Committee did not want Marie to attend the ceremony. The scientist had become embroiled in scandal because of her affair with Paul Langevin, who was married, albeit unhappily. Langevin had been a student of Pierre Curie's; he was younger than Marie, but he was, like her, a physicist. He had a solid reputation in his field and had been elected to the College de France and the Academie des Sciences. Marie and her lover rented an apartment for their secret meetings. Langevin's wife learned of the affair and threatened to expose them; three days before Marie won the second Nobel Prize, she made good on her threat.

As the wronged woman, she won the sympathy of the newspapers, which cast Marie in the role of the immoral woman. Marie was advised by a Nobel laureate to stay in France, but Albert Einstein told her that she should go to Stockholm to accept her prize. She did so, and after the ceremony, dined with the

King of Sweden. Ten days later, the Langevins went to court; his wife was given custody of the children. While they continued to share an interest in science, the publicity over the affair left its mark, and they were no longer lovers.

When 1914 came and with it the war that would redefine Europe, Marie put aside her research. With the money she'd received for her prizes, she fitted ambulances with portable X-ray machines, known as "Little Curies" to be used for the soldiers, establishing 200 X-ray installations in France and Belgium, and driving the ambulances to the front lines of battle. The year 1914 was also when the building of the Radium Institute Laboratories were completed at the University of Paris.

When World War I ended, Irene Curie joined her mother at the laboratory. The Radium Institute began to operate in earnest, becoming a center for chemistry and nuclear physics. The price of radium was prohibitively high, and the Curies decision not to patent their discovery meant that Marie was obliged to fundraise to pursue her research. An American journalist named Marie Mattingly Meloney launched a financial campaign to raise money from other American women; their goal was to bring in $100,000 to purchase a gram of radium to present to Marie Curie, by then probably the most famous woman in the world. At the time, the United States owned the largest supply of radium in the world. Robert Abbe was an American doctor who also supported the fundraising efforts. Abbe was a pioneer in the use of radium to treat cancer. The Marie Curie Radium Fund board included future First Lady Mrs. Grace Coolidge as a member, along with the wife of millionaire John D. Rockefeller. Meloney used her contact in the media world to solicit funds from ordinary magazine subscribers was well as millionaires; the funds to purchase the radium were raised, but contributions also provided money for a well-equipped laboratory.

In 1921, Marie went to the United States, where President Warren Harding presented her with a gram of pure radium to be used for research. The event took place in the East Room with more than 100 prominent scientists and diplomats from Poland and France in attendance. The radium, because of its hazardous qualities, was not brought to the ceremony. She was presented with a key to the coffer containing the radium and a Certificate for Radioactive Material from the National Bureau of Standards. The radium was subdivided into ten hermetically sealed glass tubes. Upon making the presentation, Harding said, "I have been commissioned to present to you this little phial of radium. To you we owe our knowledge and possession of it . . . confident that in your possession it will be the means further to unveil the fascinating secrets of nature, to alleviate suffering among the children of man."

Marie objected to being named the sole owner of the radium, insisting that the deed should change to pass to the laboratory instead of her family so that it would be available to other researchers.

Until the tour, Marie's daughters, who accompanied her, did not realize the extent of their mother's fame. The family was honored, interviewed and photographed. Marie received honorary degrees from the Universities of Yale, Columbia, Northwestern, Pennsylvania, and Pittsburgh. She returned to the United States in October, 1929. President Herbert

Hoover, who had been a member of the 1921 Marie Curie Radium Fund Committee, invited her to stay at the White House, an invitation that had not been offered to any previous international figures. Once again, she was feted and honored; she was honored at the 50th anniversary of the invention of the light bulb by Thomas Edison; the General Electric plant was closed in honor of her visit. She was given a bank draft to help fund research at the Radium Institute in Warsaw, Poland.

By now, she was an international scientist of renown, giving lectures in Europe and Brazil. The Curie Foundation was developed in Paris to work on medical applications for radium. In 1932, her sister Bronya became the director of the Radium Institute in Warsaw.

Radioactivity made Marie famous. It also killed her; in 1934, she died of aplastic anemia, a blood disease attributed to overexposure to radiation. People were unaware of the lethal effects of radioactivity; daughter Irene also contracted leukemia, believed to have been caused by her exposure to the levels of radioactivity that she dealt with in her work. To demonstrate how potent the levels of radioactivity are, her notebooks, years later after she used them, are still so radioactive that they can't be handled.

Why Marie Matters

The Curie family would ultimately be honored with five Nobel Prizes. In 1944, when the 96th element in the periodic table of the elements was discovered, it was named curium in her honor. While radium has a dangerous side, it's also a crucial tool in medicine, used in the treatment of cancer. The Curies received no royalties for their work on radium therapy because they had chosen not to patent their discovery. Marie's brilliant research reconfigured the fields of medicine and science. The woman who faced discrimination because of her gender is today acknowledged as a scientist who is an equal among her male peers. In 1995, the Curies' remains were taken from their original burial site and interred in the Pantheon in Paris; Marie is the only woman to receive the honor of sharing the final resting place with the most brilliant minds in France. Yet her personality remained, despite her achievements, modest. Albert Einstein said, "Marie Curie is, of all celebrated beings, the one whom fame has not corrupted."

The family honored one another's achievements; in 1924, Marie published a biography of Pierre Curie and in 1938, Eve published a biography of Marie. Eve had a poignant recollection of her mother as she wrote, "My mother was 37 years old when I was born. When I was big enough to know her, she was already an aging woman who had reached the summit of renown. And yet it is the 'celebrated scientist' who is strangest to me—probably because the idea that she was a 'celebrated scientist' did not occupy the mind of Marie Curie. It seems to me rather, that I have always lived near the poor student, haunted by dreams, who was Marie Sklodowska long before I came into the world." Eve would be lucky enough to live a very long life; she was not a scientist, which might account for her longevity. But a scientist of Marie Curie's caliber is in some ways immortal because of groundbreaking quality of her research.

Winnie Mandela the Activist 1936-

Who is Winnie Mandela?

While South African activist Nelson Mandela was under house arrest for 27 years, his wife, Winnie Madikizela-Mandela was anti-apartheid's public image, representing his leadership to the world beyond his confinement in the Victor Verster Prison. She remains a controversial figure, her image tainted by the revelation that she had been responsible for crimes of abduction, assault, torture and even murder of people who opposed her. Yet she is an inseparable part of the role that her husband played in fighting apartheid; Perhaps the bond they shared was stronger than marriage, forged in the sharing of a cause by two indomitable people who were allies as much as they were spouses. But even after their divorce in 1996, she remained part of his life, visiting him in the hospital as his life neared its end. Divorce ended the marriage; the partnership was could not be dissolved.

In the Beginning

The "Mother of her Nation" was always aware that when she was born, her mother, who had wanted a son, was disappointed. Young Winnie was a tomboy who wanted to be a doctor. But from an early age, her compassion was roused by people in need, and she would bring schoolmates home who lacked food or the money to pay their fees. Her parents, although money was hard to come by, never scolded her for bringing home the human strays.

Born 1936 in eMbongweni, in what is now the Eastern Cape Province of South Africa, Nomzamo Winifred Zanyiwe Madikizela, the future international figure, earned her degree in Johannesburg, becoming the country's first black female social worker despite the fact that blacks had limited educational opportunities during the period of government-sanctioned apartheid. She continued her studies at the University of Witwatersrand, earning a degree in international relations.

Early Influences

Winnie grew up in a world where whites and

nonwhites lived apart. Apartheid was the official policy of segregation of the races practiced by the South African government's National Party from 1948 – 1994. After the election of 1948, the residents of South Africa were classified as black, white, colored or Indian. Nonwhites were forced to live in segregated neighborhoods, denied political representation, and their citizenship was taken from them. A policy of "separate and nonequal" dominated the country as blacks received inferior medical care and educational opportunities and services. Their world was kept apart from the white world, and even beaches were segregated.

Winnie's Life Changes

At the age of 22, at a bus stop in Soweto, Winnie met her future husband in 1957. Nelson Mandela was in the process of divorcing his wife, Evelyn, with whom he had three children. They married a year later, and became the parents of two daughters. They didn't have much time together; Mandela was a lawyer and anti-apartheid activist, so it was a matter of time before arrest became a part of their marriage. He was arrested in 1963 and would spend 27 years in prison.

Knowing that her ongoing fight against the government, even more important now that she would carry it on without Mandela, would bring danger to their lives, Winnie sent her children to Swaziland to attend boarding school so that, as schoolchildren living in another country, they would have a buffer against the spotlight of their parents' battles against authority and injustice.

But during Mandela's years in prison, his wife continued to be active in the fight against apartheid, as government authorities showed no mercy toward her even though she was a woman and mother. For much of that time, she was exiled to Brandfort in the Orange Free State. After spending 18 months in solitary confinement in Pretoria Central Prison, she became well known in the West as the struggle against apartheid became an international issue. She also was subjected to torture, government surveillance, and house arrest; at one point, her home was firebombed. For her sacrifices and her struggles to combat apartheid, she, Allan Boesak and Beyers Naude were awarded the Robert F. Kennedy Human Rights Award in 1985.

Resistance to apartheid was strong, but the opposition suffered for its efforts to bring freedom to the nonwhite population that was ruled by a white minority determined to use any means to maintain power. South Africa was subjected to sanctions by the governments of the world for its policies, and in 1990, President de Klerk began the negotiating process to dismantle apartheid. In 1994, with open elections, the African National Congress led by Nelson Mandela won. But the struggle to that victory had taken decades and the suffering endured by the nonwhite population was brutal.

The fight against their shared cause was something that Winnie was able to sustain, but the separation from her husband had posed a different kind of battle, and not one that she would win. While her husband was imprisoned, Winnie was involved in an affair with another man. As for Winnie, separation would always be a factor in their relationship, and ultimately, it proved too much for the marriage, although they did not officially end their union until 1992, two years after

Mandela was released from prison. The divorce was finalized in 1996. Winnie had sought $5 million in her ex-husband's assets, which she said was half his worth, but she failed to appear for the settlement hearing and the suit was dismissed.

For Winnie, the combat against apartheid had been a consuming cause and she was not reluctant to strike out against collaborators with apartheid. She was unabashedly committed to necklacing, a practice in which a tire was doused in gasoline, placed around the neck of suspected informers, and set on fire. In 1991, she was acquitted of a charge of murder against a 14-year old boy who was accused of being an informer, she was but charged with his kidnapping; her sentence of six years in jail was appealed and ended up as a fine. A year later, the case resurfaced when the doctor who had examined the boy at Mandela's house was found murdered. In 1997, she was accused of being responsible for violations of human rights for killings and torture committed by her bodyguards, the Mandela United Football Club

Life beyond apartheid would prove to be surprisingly

difficult for Winnie Mandela. Her appointment in 1994 as Deputy Minister of Arts, Culture, Science and Technology in the newly elected government lasted less than a year as she was dismissed upon allegations of corruption.

She was sentenced to five years in prison after being charged with fraud, but was given a suspended sentence when the Pretoria High Court judge ruled that she had not committed the crimes for personal gain. The accusations cast a less than heroic light on the woman who is legitimately regarded as one of South Africa's leading figures in the struggle against apartheid. She recognized no short cuts in her task of freeing nonwhites from the grip of apartheid, and some of her methods were as ruthless as the policies she fought against. But Nelson Mandela was not always a proponent of nonviolence, and it's only fair to remember that fact when judging his wife's practices.

Years before his arrest, as the leader of the African National Congress, Nelson Mandela had abandoned peaceful protest as a means of achieving the goal of overthrowing apartheid. He was the co-founder of Umkhonto we Sizwe, which in Zulu means "Spear of the Nation" as the ANC's militant wing. The organization was banned as a terrorist group by the government, and also by the United States, for violent acts of sabotage carried out against power facilities, government posts, and for burning crops.

Ultimately, Mandela would renounce violence as a means to ending apartheid, but for his wife, the battle was not a spiritual one but a kill-or-be-killed war. Mandela's recourse to violence wasn't forgotten by history, but the memories of 27 years of imprisonment superseded the deeds of an earlier era. Winnie and her acts remained visible in the public eye.

In his will, Mandela left his assets worth $4.3 million in property and his belongings to his third wife, Graca Machal, his children, grandchildren, and great-grandchildren. There were also bequests to several educational institutions and smaller amounts to his staff and his doctors. His home in rural Qunu was, according to the will, to be used by his family in perpetuity to preserve the unity of the Mandela family.

In accordance with Xhosa tribal custom, Winnie spent a year in silent mourning following the death of Nelson Mandela. But when the year ended, the ex-wife had plenty to say, and her words would divest the past relationship of its political glamor. According to Winnie, Mandela was guilty of land fraud when he went to the Ebotwe Tribal Authority to obtain ownership of land that she says belonged to her, bypassing the authority of King Buyelekhaya Dalindyebo, who had been the one who allocated the land to her. At first, Winnie was convinced that her former husband could not have been in possession of his right mind when he made out his will.

Winnie challenged the will because she said that, under traditional African law, the property was hers and that the divorce had no bearing on her ownership. Mandela's widow waived her right to the disputed property, preferring the four properties she and Mandela had owned together, along with vehicles and jewelry Mandela had given to her. The response of the Mandelas' daughter, Zindzi, revealed that the friction within the family was not new, tweeting "Why would she expect to be maintained after his passing when she was never maintained during his lifetime?"

Why Winnie Madikizela-Mandela Matters

Winnie Mandela has been called the Mother of Her Nation for her struggles on behalf of her people. For her, serving on the front lines of apartheid politics while Mandela's 27 years of house arrest transformed him into the man who could lead South Africa past its corrosive history, there was no reconciliation. Later, she lambasted not only her ex-husband, but also Archbishop Desmond Tutu for their conciliatory gestures toward white leaders who had supported apartheid in the past. To see Nelson Mandela accepting his Nobel Peace Prize in 1993 with FW de Klerk, arouse her ire. She pointed out that de Klerk had not released Mandela from prison because of the goodness of his heart; he had done so, she said, because "the times dictated it."

In an interview in the *Evening Standard* in 2015, Winnie Mandela spoke of her disappointment in the movement. "The name Mandela is an albatross around the necks of my family. You all must realize that Mandela was not the only man who suffered. There were many others, hundreds who languished in prison and died. Many unsung and unknown heroes of the struggle, and there were others in the leadership too, like poor Steve Biko, who died of the beatings, horribly all alone."

Her daughters have occupied roles in South Africa's government. Elder daughter Zenani served as the country's ambassador to Argentina; younger daughter Zindzi occupied the position of ambassador to Denmark. Still, their mother feels that they have not taken positions in politics, or at least the political struggle as she perceives it, because they endured too much when apartheid was the cause against which her parents were fighting. The daughters of Winnie and Nelson Mandela did not have an easy upbringing; Zindzi was 18 months old when he was arrested and sentenced to life imprisonment. With their father in prison, the daughters were even more emotionally attached to their mother.

But Winnie's activism meant that the family never knew when the secret police would be at their home. There was an episode where Winnie was dragged from the home at two o'clock in the morning; she would spend the next 16 months in solitary confinement. "I never knew if she would come back alive," Zindzi

recalls. Winnie tried to provide them with as stable a childhood as possible. She would enroll them in nursery school. But when the police found out, as they always did, the principal would be intimidated and the girls would be asked to leave. Winnie tried to disguise the Mandela daughters by straightening their hair and giving them a different surname, but the police always found them. Winnie recognized that as Mandela's children, they lived their lives on an international stage.

Zindzi felt that she had to share her father with her country, and admitted that she felt bitterness that, when he was released from prison, he was not just their father. She had imagined having a home life with him and the family. "When he came out of prison we only had a few minutes with him as a family before the reception committee joined us."

When the rift developed between her parents, Zindzi took her mother's side. The world sympathized with Nelson Mandela, but while their father had become an icon under house arrest, Winnie had been on the front lines of the anti-apartheid movement, facing the

hostility of the government and its retribution. While Nelson Mandela became admired for his endurance, Winnie was larger than life. But Winnie's interpretation of Nelson's hero stance shows the cracks in the human statue.

According to his ex-wife, Mandela let his people down. "He agreed to a bad deal for the blacks," she said. "Economically, we are still on the outside. The economy is very much 'white.' It has a few token blacks, but so many who gave their life in the struggle have died unrewarded."

Another source of anger, or perhaps disappointment, for Winnie Mandela is the placement of his statue. "They put that huge statue of him right in the middle of the most affluent "white" area of Johannesburg. Not here where we spilled our blood and where it all started." Mandela because a corporation foundation, his ex-wife charged, a figurehead for the ANC to use for fundraising.

She is still relevant to the history of the anti-apartheid

movement although her political career has suffered from her brushes with the law, her outspokenness, and what might be regarded as a risky lack of judgment. She is a reminder that the battles that remain to be fought after the war has been won require different talents. Winnie Mandela did not have the skills needed for a successful politician. But she rose to meet the needs of her country when South Africa required a strong woman who could endure opposition without flinching and who would never surrender.

Hillary Clinton the Political Trailblazer 1947-

Who is Hillary Rodham Clinton?

Anyone who wants to chart the arc of Hillary Rodham Clinton's life and career can do so just by tracking the appearance of Rodham as part of her full name. She was born, grew up, and went to college as Hillary Rodham. Marriage to aspiring politician William Jefferson Clinton did not change her surname, but when her husband became governor of Arkansas and she tried out Hillary Rodham on the constituents, he lost his re-election bid. When he ran again and won, Hillary Rodham Clinton was the First Lady of Arkansas.

By the time Bill Clinton sought national office, Hillary Rodham Clinton was ready to join him; she was the first First Lady to have offices in both the West Wing and East Wing of the White House, an indication of the power-sharing that was an integral, and controversial, aspect of the Clinton marriage. Senator Hillary Rodham Clinton, presidential candidate Hillary Rodham Clinton, and Secretary of State Hillary Rodham Clinton testified to the navigation of her political fortunes but also how the public's stance had altered on the status of women. As female figures became more visible in the upper echelons of the power structure, something as insignificant as whether or not a woman kept her maiden name no longer seemed to matter.

In the Beginning

The frontrunner for the Democratic candidate for the 2016 presidential race started her life in 1947 as Hillary Diane Rodham, growing up in a suburban town in Illinois, the child of Republican parents: her father operated his own successful drapery business, her mother was a homemaker, and the family would expand to include two younger brothers. She was a

118

model student, participated in sports and Girl Scouts, graduated in the top five percent of her high school class, and was a National Merit Finalist. Both parents wanted her to have the opportunities that she deserved and didn't want her to limit herself just because she was a girl at a time when the old joke was that girls went to college to get their "Mrs." Degree.

Early Influences

Hillary Rodham cut her political teeth early, supporting Republican candidates when she was still a junior high school student. In 1964, she campaigned for anti-communist conservative Barry Goldwater, and when she went to Wellesley College in 1965, she served as president of the campus Young Republicans. But from childhood on, she had not only absorbed her family's conservative political views, but she also followed the social justice directions of her Methodist pastor and her mother.

As the 1960s turned into an era of revolt and reform, the college student found her political affiliation changing. She believed in change, but not to overthrow the systems, no matter how flawed they seemed to be.

119

Her motivation was to change what was wrong within the power structures. She supported anti-war candidate Eugene McCarthy for president and organized a student strike in support of black students at Wellesley after the assassination of Martin Luther King revealed the deep racial division in the country. College had changed her, and she was showing early signs of the political astuteness that would later brand her as a woman to watch in the changing social climate where people began to believe that, one day, a woman might be elected president of the United States.

Hillary's Life Changes

When she entered law school, she was much more than just a student. She brought her empathy along with her, not only into her classes but with her other activities as well. Her research included work on children's health and migrant worker issues. As a volunteer, she provided pro bono legal advice for low-income people, was mentored by children's rights activist Marian Wright Edelman and worked on a Senate Subcommittee chaired by Senator Walter Mondale. But the young law student wasn't studying and working all the time.

120

In 1971 she met a fellow Yale law student named Bill Clinton who came from a small town in Arkansas. She remained at Yale an extra year so that they could stay together but when he proposed marriage, she said no. Her post-Yale career found her active in the turmoil of 1970s politics. She was an advisor for the House Committee on the Judiciary, researching impeachment procedures against Richard Nixon for his role in the Watergate break-in and cover-up. Decades later, her familiarity with impeachment would take on a more personal role as her husband faced the process for his involvement with White House intern Monica Lewinsky.

But her reasons for repeatedly refusing his marriage proposals were because she feared that her career would become lost in his pursuit of his own ambitions, a challenging future for two very talented and very driven people. Finally, though, she found her way to Arkansas, where she ended up as one of two female members of the faculty of the University of Arkansas, Fayetteville School of Law. Eschewing an extravagant, elaborate wedding, Clinton and Rodham got married in the living room of the home they bought in Fayetteville.

She continued to advance in her legal career as her husband pursued his political dreams; when he became the state's governor, she acquired the title of First Lady of Arkansas. When she became a partner in the Rose Law Firm—the first female to do so—her salary was greater than her husband's. Hillary Rodham gave birth to the couple's only child, a daughter they named Chelsea, in 1980; that same year, Bill Clinton lost the election for governor. In 1982, he won the office again, and Hillary Rodham Clinton again assumed the role of First Lady.

Bill Clinton turned his sights to the White House in a campaign that was rife with gossip about rumored infidelities. Hillary's acerbic comments in interviews about not being a wife who stayed home baking cookies rubbed some voters the wrong way, creating a hostility that would linger for a long time. But in 1993, the Clintons moved to the White House, where the President made no secret of his respect for his wife's judgment. However, the country was not yet ready for what it regarded as a co-presidency and when the First Lady was put in charge of advancing the cause of health care reform, the proposal failed. She turned her attention to women's rights both at home and abroad. She continued her advocacy for children by promoting nationwide immunization against childhood illnesses. She urged women to get regular mammograms to detect breast cancer. She didn't ignore the men, either; she supported efforts to increase funding for research for prostate cancer at the National Institutes of Health. She was also involved in finding out more about Gulf War Syndrome and the illnesses affecting veterans of the first Gulf War.

She became a lightning rod for controversy, but investigations failed to turn up evidence of criminal misconduct. But the scandal that would mar the Clinton presidency was exposed in 1998 when the public learned that the president had been sexually involved with White House intern Monica Lewinsky. However, his marriage remained intact and so did his presidency despite his impeachment, and when he left office in 2001, his approval ratings were high.

It was the other Clinton's turn. She was elected to two terms as New York's junior senator, where she surprised veteran members of the Senate with her low-key, hardworking approach to legislation. She continued her interest in health by investigating the issues faced by the first responders to the 9/11 attacks. Adopting the concerns of her new state home, she was able to secure billions in funding to redevelop the site where the World Trade Center had been destroyed. She helped introduce legislation that increased the size of the regular army by 80,000 soldiers when she realized that deployments were debilitating both regular and reserve forces.

In 2008, she announced that she was a candidate for the office her husband had held for two terms, president of the United States. The campaign was competitive and her chief rival was Senator Barack Obama of Illinois. But the African-American senator ran a smoother, more cohesive campaign than his more experienced rival, and in June, she ended her candidacy and endorsed Obama's run for the White House. Despite losing the primary campaign, Clinton had blazed a spectacular political trail, with more than 17 million votes, the most votes and delegates won by a woman.

When Obama won the election, he had one candidate in mind for Secretary of State: Hillary Rodham Clinton. Insiders revealed that the president-to-be was fascinated by the "team of rivals" that Abraham Lincoln assembled in his Cabinet when he was elected in 1861. Opting for the best candidate for the position rather than the most loyal, Obama made it known that the position was hers if she wanted it. At first reluctant, she gave up her Senate seat to join the Obama administration, setting another first: the only former First Lady who would occupy a seat in a presidential cabinet.

Just as she had been notable for traveling as First Lady, Hillary tallied many miles in the cause of diplomacy. The world view of the United States following the aggressive policies of the Bush presidency meant that she needed to focus on repairing the country's reputation in diplomatic circles. She worked to develop the Global Hunger and Food Security Program so that the needs of poor countries could be addressed. She was not afraid to support the use of military force when she felt it was needed; nor was she hesitant to pursue diplomatic solutions to problems that needed words rather than bullets. She was tireless in advancing the cause of women's rights all over the world, and when she left the position after President Obama was re-elected, she had visited 112 countries. She has been criticized for failing to effect significant, concrete changes during her tenure, but Hillary felt that the roots of her work would need time to grow before results were perceived.

As soon as she left the Obama White House, everyone from pundits to pollsters speculated on her presidential ambitions, but Hillary refused to confirm their theories. That is, until April 12, 2015, when she sent out an email announcing that she was running for the office of president in the 2016 election.

When the campaign for the presidency got underway, the most experienced candidate was Hillary Clinton. The Republican campaign was dominated by outsiders; Donald Trump, the outspoken, belligerent real estate titan and Ben Carson, the conservative neurosurgeon, would seem to be polar opposites, and in fact they are.

But the initial months of the campaign brought no halt to their preeminence, and candidates with more traditional political backgrounds such as Senators Ted Cruz, Marco Rubio and Lindsay Graham, struggled to create a definitive image for the electorate.

In 2014, while she was still Secretary of State, Hillary Clinton enjoyed a personal event when daughter Chelsea gave birth to Charlotte Clinton Mezvinsky. But when the grandmother awaiting the birth of a granddaughter is Hillary Clinton, the personal becomes political. Clinton told an audience that one of the nurses thanked her for fighting for paid leave. Her role as a grandmother would become part of her political arsenal as she spoke to audiences on behalf of the issues which mattered the most to her. Speaking to an audience during her campaign, Clinton said, "I want every child, every child in our country, and not just the granddaughter of a former President or a former secretary of stae, but every child to have the chance to live up to his or her God-given potential."

Her status as a grandmother is, in itself, momentous for a political leader like Hillary Clinton. While some believe that she needs a softening of her image in order to appeal to voters, others have noted that to be both a grandmother and a political candidate in a country where older women do not always command respect is in itself groundbreaking.

Although Clinton has served as the first lady of Arkansas and the United States, a senator from New York, and Secretary of State, her political credentials have continued to be questioned by her opponents.

Hillary Rodham Clinton's image has been defined over the years even as her political resume has evolved. As the year 2015 came to a close, and the specter of terrorism, which has never really abated since the September 11 attacks by al-Qaeda, once again dominated the voters' fears, her experience in foreign affairs stood her in good stead. She was called before to testify about her role in the attacks on the U.S. embassy in Benghazi, Libya, when four Americans, including Ambassador Christopher Stevens, were killed by Islamic militants in 2012.

When she appeared before the House Select Committee on Benghazi, she impressed viewers with her composure through 11 hours of testifying about the decisions she made during her tenure as the Secretary of State. Her Republican interrogators insisted that the hearing was not about her, but its purpose was to find out the truth about what happened at Benghazi, Libya. However, the motives of the committee were cast into doubt when Republican House Majority Leader Kevin McCarthy boasted that the success of the Republicans in keeping the Benghazi episode in the public eye had brought down her poll numbers. As the new hearing was about to get underway, another Republican, Representative Richard Hanna, admitted that the purpose of the hearing was to "go after people and an individual, Hillary Clinton."

Both the Republicans and Hillary Clinton had something to prove, and the testimony was in some ways about the 2016 election. Casting doubts on Clinton's leadership would harm her candidacy. Clinton's measured answers to questions that have been repeatedly asked shed no new light on the Benghazi attack, but it did demonstrate that the Democratic candidate for president possesses ample amounts of self-control and stamina. These traits are valued in a president, and in a commander-in-chief.

Speculation about her ability to lead the nation inevitably drifts to the question of, should she become president, what will the role be for her husband, the former president, a man who is hardly known for remaining on the sidelines? What would his title be? The title of "First Gentleman" is commonly used when married female leaders are in office in the states. Clinton treated the question with humor when late-night host Jimmy Kimmel asked her what Bill Clinton would be called in her White House. She acknowledged that it would be complicated because her husband is still referred to as "Mr. President" by many, offering "first dude," "first mate," and the aforementioned "first gentleman" as suggestions. But the real issue in the event that she becomes president is the matter of what role her husband would play in her presidency.

It was no secret during Bill Clinton's two terms in office that he relied upon his wife's advice. He would certainly fill that position if their situations reverse and she is the one for whom *Hail to the Chief* is playing. Friends and colleagues speculate that he would avoid the spotlight during the early stages of his wife's occupation of the Oval Office so that there's no doubt about who is running the country. He could serve credibly as an envoy on missions to other countries, bringing with him the stature of his former presidency and the influence of his position as the spouse of the president. Clinton's insights into political strategy and his connection to the public will always be assets as long as there is a Clinton running for public office.

Whether she wins the election to become the 45th president and the first female president of the United States or not, her position as one of the most influential women of this century is secure. She has completely refurbished the traditional political life by her actions as a political wife, refuting the saying by F. Scott Fitzgerald that there are no second acts in American lives.

The curtain has not yet come down on the political life of Hillary Rodham Clinton.

Benazir Bhutto the Political Pioneer of Pakistan 1953-2007

1426

Who was Benazir Bhutto?

Pakistan may not be noted for its liberal endorsement of women in politics, but any assessment of the country must take note of the fact that Benazir Bhutto was elected to two terms as the country's prime minster; the only female prime minster the country has ever had, and the only female prime minister of a Muslim nation. Countries which boast of equality for their women have not necessarily followed up that claim with female representation in the executive governing branch. Benazir's career included political accomplishments partnered with charges of corruption, and advances that were matched ultimately by assassination. She blazed particularly unique paths in her rise to power and subsequent generations of women will recognize the sacrifices that she made in order to support the cause of democracy in her country.

In the Beginning

Cynics may assert that Benazir Bhutto's political advancement was the result of nepotism. She was the eldest daughter of Zulfikar Ali Bhutto and Begum Nusrat Ispahani, whose Kurdish descent proved to be an asset in the family's political success. The Bhutto household was multilingual, but English was Benazir's preferred language; her Urdu was not as proficient, or at least as formal, as her English. Growing up in the milieu of government power, similar to the role that India's first female prime minister, Indira Gandhi, played in her father's household, she was keenly aware of the political scene in Pakistan.

Early Influences

After a convent education in Pakistan, she attended Harvard's Radcliffe College, graduating cum laude with a degree in comparative government. While a student, she absorbed her education in democracy as well, and described her years at school as the happiest years of her life. She followed her bachelor's degree with classes at Oxford University in Great Britain, studying courses in international law, diplomacy, philosophy, politics, and economics. She achieved an honor which was a forecast of her future career when she became the first Asian woman to be elected president of the Oxford Union, the university's debating society. But the controversy that would always envelope her was also a part of her student career, due to the unpopularity of her father's politics.

Benazir's Life Changes

A military coup against her father in 1977 brought General Muhammad Zia-ul-Haq to power as prime minster, and along with it, a military dictatorship to Pakistan. Benazir Bhutto and her brother were not excluded from the fallout, spending a year and a half in and out of house arrest as they led the opposition's effort to force General Zia to drop the charge of murder that had been leveled against their father, the former prime minister. Their efforts were in vain, and the jailed prime minister was hanged in 1979 while the Bhutto family was maintained in a police camp for a month after the execution.

Although local elections had led to victory for the Pakistan Peoples Party (PPP) which Bhutto had founded, Zia postponed the national elections and sent Benazir, her younger brother Murtaza, and their mother to the Larkana Central Jail, the seventh time in the two years following Zia's coup that the trio had been arrested. When she was sentenced to six month's imprisonment in the Sukkur Jail, in a cell in the desert, she suffered from boils, invasive insects and the terrible heat. Her hair fell out in handfuls, and layers of skin peeled off her hands. She ended up in the hospital, and then was sent to Karachi Central Jail, where she remained until December, 1981. House arrest for over two years followed.

When her family was released by Zia in 1984 in order to receive medical treatment abroad, Benazir did not allow distance to stifle her political activism. She became the leader in exile of the PPP, the first time that a Pakistani woman was named to the leadership of a major political party. Distance may have been what saved their lives; in 1985, Benazir's brother Shahnawaz was poisoned. Convinced that the murder was at the hands of Zia, the family in Britain went into hiding.

Despite the pressure that the PPP exerted on Zia from abroad, Zia remained in power. But the international world was also exerting pressure and he was forced to hold an election. Because the election didn't conform to the requirements of Pakistan's Constitution, Benazir urged a boycott of the election. She denounced Zia in speeches when she addressed the European Parliament in 1985; her act resulted in death sentences back home against 54 members of the PPP.

Amidst all the activism on behalf of the PPP, Bhutto found time for marriage; she and Asif Ali Zardari were married in December, 1987, when she was 34 years old. The couple would have three children, a son and two daughters. The marriage surprised many who expected Bhutto to adopt as independent a role in matrimony as she had in her political career. The marriage was arranged by her mother and Bhutto met her husband five days before the engagement was announced. The marriage to the wealthy businessman and polo player had been negotiated by her family members; Bhutto explained that she consented to the marriage in recognition of her religious obligations and her duty to her family.

While conceding that her decision would come as a

surprise to her Western friends, Bhutto explained that she did not have the normal social opportunities of other women. Had she opted to pursue a romantic attachment on her own, she would have been subject to speculation that would have abetted Zia and his political agenda. In a telephone interview with the New York Times, she said, "In a Moslem society, it's not done for women and men to meet each other, so it's very difficult to get to know each other, and, my being the leader of the largest opposition party in Pakistan, it would have been a lot of rumor to the grist and bad for the image if I had chosen another course." Although the marriage was an arranged one, Bhutto was permitted to approve or disapprove of the candidate chosen by her family, and she noted that Zardari's tolerance indicated that he would not be troubled by being married to a woman with her own career.

That career was soon to rise to greater heights. After Zia died in a plane crash in 1988, the PPP won seats when the first open general elections in over ten years were held. As the PPP chairperson, Benazir Bhutto would become Pakistan's Prime Minister, three months after giving birth to her first child. In her speech to the crowd following her election, Benazir evoked the memory of her days in America when she called the people together in celebration of democracy and what she described as "the three most beautiful words in the English language: "We the people."

One of the ways in which Bhutto combined a tribute to her father with acknowledgment of the way in which her upbringing had allowed her to achieve a level of education denied to most women in her country was by the establishment of the Shaheed Zulfikar Ali Bhutto Institute of Science and Technology in Karachi, Islamabad, Hyderabad and Larkana. The students pursue learning in computer engineering, law, media studies and other disciplines that allow females to obtain professional training in modern fields.

But she found that governing was much more challenging than campaigning. The effects of the domestic policies that Zia had sown were part of Bhutto's harvest to reap, causing economic problems. Originally allied with the United States as mutual allies against communism, Bhutto's concern at the American support of the Afghan mujahedeen following the

Soviet invasion of Afghanistan would prove prescient. The U.S. was alarmed at the Pakistani nuclear weapons program, and the alliance ended in 1990. She attempted to improve the tense relations with long-term enemy India, negotiating a trade agreement and welcoming the Indian premier in a visit to Pakistan.

Benazir was defeated in the election of 1990 and was accused of misconduct. She left the country and was convicted of corruption. Although she was sentenced to a three-year prison term, Benazir remained the leader of the PPP and was actively engaged in the party's politics.

When President Musharraf granted Benazir amnesty on all the charges that had been made against her, she returned to Pakistan in 2007. At the homecoming rally to celebrate her return, a suicide bombing killed 136 people. Musharraf called a state of emergency and placed her under house arrest. When the state of emergency was lifted a month later, Bhutto returned to campaigning. This time, she would not be lucky when the suicide bomber attacked; she and 28 others were killed just after she had addressed her supporters at a rally that attracted thousands. According to the government spokesman, Benazir wasn't killed by gunfire, but by hitting her head on the sunroof of her vehicle. The prime minister claimed that her death was her own fault for failing to take proper precautions in a campaign that she knew was dangerous.

Accusations were made against Prime Minister Perez Musharraf for failing to provide his political adversary with sufficient security. Other accusations against him included charges that he was actually complicit in the assassination plot. In 2007, a Pakistani court indicted the former general, who rose to power through a military coup, on murder and conspiracy charges connected with Bhutto's death. The indictment did not implicate him in the assassination, however. The accusation was that his government was inexcusable in its failure to provide Bhutto with sufficient security; the charge also documented a military cover-up in the investigation.

Bhutto was aware of the risks of her political campaign. She had prepared an email to CNN reporter Wolf Blitzer, to be sent by a friend only if Bhutto were killed, which affirmed that Musharraf's actions and those that she referred to as his "minions" had left her feeling insecure for her safety.

Ultimately Musharraf would fall from power as the politics of Pakistan continued to reveal the country's turmoil. But the truth about who was behind the assassination plot against the world's first Muslim prime minister remains unknown.

Why Benazir Bhutto Matters

Asian politics has seen its share of female leaders: India, the Philippines, Bangladesh, Indonesia, of Sri Lanka, Australia, and South Korea have witnessed women rising to the highest elected positions in their countries, so Benazir Bhutto was by no means a solitary female in power. For many of these women, their ascent to power and influence was accompanied by social upheaval, violence, and even murder. Women may be regarded as the gentler sex but the response to their political status has hardly been chivalric.

Pakistan since Bhutto's death has been an unsettled

nation gripped between the fist of religious extremism that would prefer to see women return to secondary status and a tradition of education and equality for females. Bhutto was not raised to be subjugated. But her legacy lives on. Pakistani girls have a path to follow if they wish to rise to political power; the pathway will not be a smooth one, but no amount of ideological dogma can erase the fact that in the twentieth century, Pakistan elected a female prime minister.

Despite her death, Bhutto found a way to provide the means for women to realize that their goals and dreams are just as valid as male aspirations. The Benazir Income Support program distributes funding to low-income families in the country with no conditions. In 2013, approximately 5.5 million people receive a supplementary amount of $24 twice a month, which is generally spent to feed their families. Developed by Bhutto with Pakistani economist Dr. Kaiseer Bengali, the program went from vision to reality after Bhutto died, when her husband, President Asif Ali Zardari, named the program in her memory. The funds are deposited into the bank account of a female, not a male, in the household, empowering poor Pakistani women and bestowing upon them the respect due to someone who makes financial decisions. The administrative requirements put in place—the women must obtain national identity cards and open a bank account—help females to acquire a fiscal identify in a nation where the births and deaths of its female citizens are often not registered in the official records.

Female education remains a priority in Pakistan. The Bhutto daughters, Asifa and Bakhtawar, received a university education and continue their mother's trailblazing by encouraging Pakistani women to pursue their education so that they can fulfill their potential and become a beneficial force in the nation's future.

Anyone who doubts that Bhutto, despite her death, has served as a role model for Pakistani females has failed to recognize the generation to which the torch has been passed. Malala Yousafzai, a young Pakistani schoolgirl of 15, was intentionally shot by a Taliban gunman in 2012. The gunman, upon asking her name as she boarded a school bus on her way to school, aimed his gun at her head and pulled the trigger. Following the violent attack, Pakistani cities erupted in protest; millions signed a petition distributed by the Right to Education campaign. The first Right to

Education bill was ratified shortly after.

Yousafzai names Bhutto as an idol, and wore her white shawl in 2013 when she addressed the United Nations. Gunfire may be the extremist's way to try to stop the empowerment of women and the advances of education, but it did not kill the young girl, who went on to become, in 2014, the youngest recipient of the Nobel Peace Prize when she was 17. The young Muslim girl who is an advocate for the rights of children and women, is an international figure and has refused to allow death threats to impede her crusade. Without the prior example of Benazir Bhutto, her zeal may not have been able to rise above the traditional tradition which the Taliban expects of its females.

The female leaders of arch-enemies India and Pakistan, Indira Gandhi and Benazir Bhutto, both met their deaths at the hands of assassins. They knew the risks when they began their work in politics. Benazir Bhutto was not a sheltered daughter; she was well aware, as the scion of a dominant political family that she was traveling on a perilous journey. It was challenging enough to be a male leader in a country such as

Pakistan, where her father was ousted in a coup and hanged. But to be a woman in the highest echelons of influence in countries where democracy is still young, or worse, fragile, and to have accepted the vicissitudes of a political life, argues a level of courage that male leaders have not always had to summon. But as women advance in countries that have historically limited their opportunities, generations to come will walk in their footsteps.

Conclusion

Eve's fall from grace came from biting into a piece of fruit that was forbidden to her. But it's also possible to assess her as a woman who craved knowledge that was denied to her. For the daughters of Eve, knowledge, power, and freedom would not be theirs for the asking. They would have to fight for those things. Perhaps Eve's role can be evaluated metaphorically rather than just theologically. She was curious, she sought information that was forbidden to her, and she was punished. Women who, throughout the centuries, have done the same have also paid the price for aspiring to roles which tradition decreed should be solely occupied by men. And yet the persistence of the females in this book demonstrates that whatever one may say of the so-called "weaker sex," the X chromosome is not an indicator of defeat. It has been a long, strife-filled climb to equality and the victory is far from won. But women cannot be discounted as partners in the decision-making process by which nations govern, go to war, raise children, and conduct themselves in a world which is vastly different from the one their great-grandmothers would have recognized at the start of the previous generations.

The twentieth century began with women fighting for the right to vote and facing scorn and adversity for daring to think that they could presume to have the wisdom to take part in government. But women had already passed that litmus test: Cleopatra, Isabella, and Victoria were born to thrones. Cleopatra has been judged as a romantic character more often than she's assessed as a queen, as if her dalliance with Caesar and union with Mark Antony disqualified her from genuine leadership. Isabella and Victoria, the former a queen with genuine power, the latter a constitutional monarch, set their mark upon their countries as resolutely as any of the kings who ruled before them or after.

As royalty waned and democracy spread, the pathway to power traveled not through blue-blooded veins but through elections. In different ways, Benazir Bhutto and Winnie Mandela persevered against the entrenched powers that held an iron grip on authority and refused to share power. Death and dishonor was their ultimate fate, and the blinding light of history reveals that they were not blameless, but they deserve credit for the astonishing courage they displayed as they faced down political adversity. The fight for freedom to which Juana Azurduy dedicated her life was consuming and fierce, yet it took over a century before her contributions were evaluated as part of the liberation process which freed South America from colonial rule. In the spheres of literature and science, Mary Wollstonecraft and Marie Curie faced senseless prejudice as they fought to use their talents in pursuit of knowledge.

Inevitably, we must wonder what the world would have been like had the unknown, unnamed women of the past been offered the opportunity to develop their abilities and take their place in positions of power and leadership. Who are those females of the centuries before who possessed intelligence and will, but lacked the opportunity to show what they were made of? Today's women benefit from the sacrifices of a gender that, once upon a dark time, had to accept sacrifice as a result of their sex. But although the glass ceiling continues to exist, it is cracking.

The modern political stage has been enlivened by the drama of Hillary Rodham Clinton, who has matured in the public eye from the embattled First Lady to the diligent senator and the internationally admired secretary of state. Where her quest for the presidency will take her remains to be seen, but as she campaigns, shakes hands, kisses babies and gives interviews, she will not have to listen to doubters claim that women don't have the skills to be leaders. The annals of history are rich with those who went before her, who were doubted, and who triumphed over their naysayers.

**** PREVIEW OTHER BOOKS BY THIS AUTHOR****

[Excerpt from the first 2 Chapters – for complete book, please purchase on Amazon.com]

"MEN THAT CHANGED THE COURSE OF HISTORY" by Dominique Atkinson

Introduction

The 21st century stands witness to the achievements of some of the most influential men in the world. And yet, no matter how today's movers and shakers stand in contemporary rankings, how can we compare them to the giants of the past, the men who took history in their bare hands and bent it to their will? Whether they strode upon the stages of military power or at the altars of religious belief, they have left their marks on civilization.

Accustomed as we are to the rule of law, we risk forgetting that the legend of Moses the Lawgiver and his acquisition of the Ten Commandments is the landmark event in Jewish pre-history. Those original stone tablets have been the midwife to numerous judicial children, blending the obligations of moral law with the requirements of civil and criminal law in a succinct body.

Bill Gates and Microsoft transformed the way in which data could be collected and compiled; when Gates retired to leave his desktop empire behind in favor of philanthropy, was it because he was ready for a new phase in his life or was it because, as the legend says of Alexander the Great, there were no worlds left to conquer?

How would Constantine's predecessor, Julius Caesar, have reacted if he'd known that over 300 years after his reign, a subsequent emperor would turn his back on the Roman gods and embrace Christianity, a religion that began with the ministry of an obscure carpenter from an insignificant region of the empire and evolved into a faith practiced by billions? And,

151

centuries later, how does the upstart Corsican Napoleon rank as the military leader who created an empire with himself as its head, reminiscent of Caesar, and redesigned his nation?

How do the advances made by cell phone technology that have been so integral to the Apple empire founded by the late Steve Jobs compare to the letters, journeys, and missionary zeal of Saint Paul, who traveled with that obscure carpenter's story across thousands of miles, braving shipwrecks, pirates, prison, and ultimately, execution?

What was the force in the desert that stirred up the Prophet Mohammed and inspired the birth of a religion whose believers will make up more than an estimated 50 percent of the population in 50 countries?

The names of these men have echoed through the halls of history since their exploits reconfigured the maps, laws, beliefs, and annals of the past. Today we live in a world shaped by their footprints. But what do we know of these game-changers? Immersed as we are in social media, headlines, 24-hour news and the Internet, how can we effectively evaluate the parts that these men played when they occupied the stage of world events?

Chapter One: Moses the Lawgiver

Who was Moses?
Moses never went to law school. Nor did he have any prior experience as a tour guide. It's obvious that the man who led his travelers on a 40-year journey through the wilderness lacked a GPS; cynics might even say that he lacked any sense of direction. But Moses was not appointed by God to lead the people of Israel because of his navigational skills. He was charged not only with freeing an enslaved people but with forging them into a nation: 12 tribes with a primitive awareness of one deity, transformed into a people whose commitment to the law and to monotheism would give them the skills they would need to survive in a world that all too often proved hostile.

Moses stands tall in an ancient time when men and myth frequently merged, until the saga becomes embedded in truth, regardless of what can be proven. Archeologists, historians, and theologians cannot reach a consensus about the man who is revered by the three major monotheistic religions of Judaism, Christianity, and Islam. His life is estimated to have taken place as long ago as 1500 years before the birth of Jesus Christ, but a man of this stature bestows upon the millennia a sense of eternity because his legacy, the Ten Commandments, is as relevant now as when the tablets first appeared.

It's not as though there were no laws before Moses. After all, Hammurabi's Code established a legal system for the Babylonians approximately several centuries before Moses is estimated to have made his appearance. However, Hammurabi's legal doctrine was more of a civil structure than Moses' laws, which were based upon the moral code ordained by God. Viewed in another light, there are no Hollywood movies starring A-list actors telling the story of Hammurabi. *Exodus*, the story of Moses starring Christian Bale, was a Hollywood blockbuster. And before Bale, there was Charlton Heston taking on the role of the Hebrew leader in The Ten *Commandments*. But who is the character of Moses outside of today's silver screen and the Bible?

In the Beginning

Moses entered history in the Old Testament Book of Exodus at a time when his people, the Israelites, who went to Egypt generations before to escape a famine, had been downgraded from royal favorites to royal slaves. The Egyptian pharaoh, fearing that the fertility of the Israelites would overwhelm the population of his country, decided upon a ruthless solution. The midwives were ordered by the pharaoh to let infant girls live, but to kill the boys. The Bible says that the midwives obeyed God, and refused to kill the baby boys. Their response, when asked by the pharaoh why the Israelites continued to have male children, was that Hebrew women gave birth before the midwives arrived.

A modern saying asserts that behind every great man is a great woman. Moses' early life was a testimonial to these words because his very existence depended upon the courage of women: first the brave midwives who risked pharaoh's ire to protect the children they delivered, and then his mother Jochebed, who defied the decree. When her baby boy was born, the Book of

Exodus tells us that she placed her son in a basket in the reeds on the banks of the Nile. When the pharaoh's daughter went to bathe in the river, she found the basket and adopted the baby, naming him Moses, an Egyptian and not a Hebrew name. Exodus relates that Moses' older sister Miriam, conveniently on site when the baby was discovered, offered to find an Israelite nurse for the baby. The royal infant's biological mother was the nurse; it's easy to see that Moses came from a most resourceful family, with female relatives who knew how to maneuver in a dangerous world. That resourcefulness would stand Moses in good stead in the years to come.

Early Influences

As a member of the royal household, Moses lived a life of privilege. We know nothing of those early years, although cinematic accounts have created scenes which, while entertaining, fail to fill in the gaps. However, he was aware of his own heritage, and knew that he was not an Egyptian by birth. What we do know is that, one day, when Moses saw an Egyptian beating an Israelite, he lost his temper—Moses' temper would get the better of him more than once—and killed the Egyptian. His act was not appreciated by his people; when Moses tried to break up a fight between two Israelite slaves, one of the men challenged him by asking him if he intended to kill him as he had the Egyptian.

Moses had not concealed his act as well as he thought. Some scholars believe that when Moses was an adult, the ruling pharaoh was Thutmose III, a brilliant military tactician with a history of ruthless actions. Moses apparently felt—correctly, as it turned out—that his quasi-royal status would not save him from the wrath of the pharaoh. With his life in danger from the pharaoh, Moses fled from Egypt and made his way to Midian in northwestern Arabia.

Moses began a new life in a new land. He had made a good impression by coming to the rescue of seven young women when shepherds tried to prevent them from watering their flocks of sheep. Moses married Zipporah, one of the seven, and began a family. His life must have seemed a far cry from his daily routine in Midian, but his destiny seemed to be decided; he was a husband, a father, a shepherd. But the situation in Egypt had not changed, even though he was no longer a part of it; although he was distant from the scene, the cruelty to the Israelites had only increased.

157

Moses' Life Changes

One day, while tending to his father-in-law's flocks, Moses had a visit from a being whose status surpassed anything at the Egyptian court. He saw a bush on fire, but he could tell that nothing was burning. Intrigued, Moses went closer. But not too close—a voice from the bush told him not to come nearer because he was on holy ground. And then came an introduction that was to change the course of history. "I am the God of your father, the God of Abraham, the God of Isaac, and the God of Jacob." Frightened, Moses hid his face.

God then proceeded to conduct one of the most unusual job interviews ever recorded. Moses, God said, was to go to Egypt and rescue the Israelite slaves so that he could bring them to freedom in a prosperous new land. Moses wanted to know, logically enough, why he was the one to do this task. God answered the question behind the question, telling Moses that God would be with him. But Moses was by no means easy to convince. He reminded God that God had been a stranger to the Israelites; they would need to be introduced. God provided the introductory information. But Moses proved his mettle by continuing to probe God. What if they didn't believe that Moses was sent by God? He reminded God that he wasn't eloquent (Moses was said to stutter). Moses asked how he could convince the Israelites that he was sent by God to deliver them from the Egyptians.

Suddenly it was God who had to present his credentials. He transformed Moses' staff into a serpent and then back into a staff; he afflicted Moses' hand with leprosy and then healed it. But Moses didn't capitulate, another trait that would serve him well when he was facing an intransigent monarch in Egypt. Moses explained again that he wasn't a smooth talker; he would need help if he were to take on this mission. Finally, God agreed to allow Moses' older brother Aaron to accompany Moses on this mission.

Aaron was Moses' intermediary with the Israelites, convincing them that God intended to rescue them from bondage. But the pharaoh was not so obliging. Stubbornly he refused to release his slaves, even though his land was cursed by a series of plagues. Until the last, terrible, inevitable plague. The tenth plague sent the Angel of Death to the households of the Egyptians but passed over the Israelite homes, an event commemorated in the symbolic holiday of

159

Passover. Grieving at the death of his heir and the monumental loss of life, the pharaoh released the Israelites from captivity and they began their journey from enslavement to freedom under Moses' leadership. But then the pharaoh changed his mind, called for his warriors and chariots, galloped off in pursuit of his escaping slaves, and nearly overtook them. Then Moses raised his staff, and the waters of the Red Sea parted, allowing the Israelites to cross on dry land. But when the Egyptians followed, the walls of water engulfed them and they drowned.

Life, however, would prove to be very different on the other side of the sea, as Moses became a full-time nanny to a people who had grown so accustomed to enslavement that, instead of rejoicing in their liberation, they berated their liberator because their meals no longer had the same seasonings and flavor as those they enjoyed in Egypt. For the sake of a good meal, it seemed, the Israelites were ready to relinquish their freedom.

Their complaints and accusations sorely tried Moses' patience. It became Moses' task to teach the former slaves that with freedom came responsibility, both to one another and to God. He went up to Mount Sinai to receive the stone tablets upon which were written the laws that God had decreed his people were to live by.

Moses' leadership encompassed a variety of roles as the Israelites made their way from slavery to freedom. But God had told Moses that he would not be the one to take the people to their new homeland. The prophet who taught his people to be a nation died on Mount Nebo, where legend says that his grave was dug by God. For the Jews, no other prophet compares to him.

Why Moses Matters

Moses received the Ten Commandments from God; the first four commandments are based on religion; the fifth commandment concerns family responsibility; the sixth and eighth address the crimes of murder and theft; the seventh, ninth, and tenth focus on moral living: don't commit adultery, don't lie, and don't covet the belongings of others. It's a succinct body of law, but from it comes the foundation of our concept of justice and morality. The books of Deuteronomy and Leviticus provided more detailed laws for living as a people, but it's the Ten Commandments that altered history. They came down from Mount Sinai, they were held intact along with Christian precepts that would come much later. They traveled across oceans and seas, and took root in countries and continents far distant from the land of milk and honey where the Israelites would claim a home.

The legacy of Moses is lasting. The American Supreme Court pays tribute to Moses the Lawgiver. Above the back entrance where the Supreme Court meets, Moses is one of three figures in the frieze, taking his place in history for his bequest to humanity; he's holding blank tablets which bring to mind the Ten Commandments. Throughout the world, as laws are made and challenged, the contribution of Moses to the vitality of both legal courts and personal conscience remains a bulwark of jurisprudence.

Chapter Two: Alexander the Great

Who was Alexander?

Alexander, the Great never went to military school. But he had a pedigree that would be the envy of any West Point cadet, and a claim to fame that four-star generals would covet. This martial wunderkind was never defeated in battle. His native Macedon's boundaries were unable to contain him; Alexander conquered much of what was regarded as the known world at the time: Egypt, Mesopotamia, Anatolia, Syria, Phoenicia, Judea, and Gaza, reaching as far as India and covering 3000 miles of land. The only reason that his conquests ended at India was because his troops had had enough of wandering and battle, and they wanted to return home.

In the Beginning

Home was Macedon. His father Philip II was the king of Macedon; it was his principal wife, one of a handful of women also married to Philip, who gave birth to Alexander, on a memorable day when her husband had been victorious in battle. To make it a trifecta, Philip's horses had also been victorious, winning at the Olympic Games. The queen decided that her son's birth, her husband's battle triumph, and Olympic laurels merited a personal response. So she gave herself a new name. Born Polyxena, she had named herself Myrtale when she joined a cult, but Alexander's mother is most commonly known as Olympias, the name taken in honor of the king's victory at the Olympic Games of 356 BCE.

163

All of which sounds worthy of celebration, but the truth is that Alexander's royal parents were a tempestuous pair. Had they lived in modern times, their marriage would have made the front pages of the tabloids. As it was, Philip's infidelities and Olympias' jealousy attracted sufficient notice to become notorious, creating reputations that have lasted for centuries.

Early Influences

As a royal prince, he was smart enough—the legendary philosopher Aristotle was his tutor from age 13 to 16 years—and privileged enough to have chosen an easier life had he wanted to do so. But nobility in those ancient times did not necessarily promise a life of ease. In order to maintain what he was destined to inherit, he would need to defend it. The tempo of the times also meant that a leader had to expect that his lands would be coveted by others; a nation which had a powerful military man on the throne seemed more likely to thrive.

Philip was a warrior, and he would expect his son to follow his lead. But Alexander's gifts were not merely

164

military. From an early age Alexander became the stuff of legend, some coming from a time when it was easy to believe that a youth so gifted was surely the offspring of the gods, perhaps even Zeus himself (a tale that might have flattered Olympias, but not necessarily Philip), and others from the boy's own remarkable exploits.

Nearly as famous as Alexander is his horse. The story says that one day, a trader brought a horse to court to sell, but the horse refused to accept a rider. No one could mount him. Recognizing such a beast as useless for his purposes, King Philip lost interest. But ten-year old Alexander proved himself to be an observant boy; he had noticed that the horse was frightened of its own shadow. Through careful training, gaining the horse's trust, and patience unusual in a child of that age, Alexander was able to mount and ride him. This stamina and insight would serve him well as the horse Bucephalus bore his master into battle in lands far from Macedon.

At 16, Alexander's education ended. Aristotle had taught him, as well as the youths who would become his generals, well. Alexander himself was a voracious reader, but the Greek philosopher also taught his students lessons which reflected the broad and expansive regard for knowledge which was characteristic of the Athenians: they learned philosophy and logic, science, ethics, art, and medicine.

From the classroom, Alexander went to the battlefield, and when there was a revolt against the king, it was the king's son who put it down and named a city after himself, one of 70 that would bear his name. One of those cities would be Alexandria in Egypt, which would eventually be second in size only to Rome. Father and son went to war against their foes, defeating the Athenians and the Thebans and establishing an alliance with the intention of going to war against the mighty Persian Empire.

Father and son were brothers-in-arms, but as father and son, their relationship was often stormy. Alexander's position as heir depended upon his father's intention to keep him so, but also upon the absence of another claimant. Philip's marriage to a young woman of childbearing age brought those possibilities home when the bride's uncle, who also happened to be Philip's general, became drunk and, speaking unwisely, as wedding guests have done since time immemorial, voiced his hope that his niece would give birth to an heir. Not the kind of wedding toast that the current heir was likely to welcome. Alexander, along with his mother, Olympias, escaped from Macedon, but Alexander returned six months later when father and son had had time to calm down.

Alexander's Life Changes

Weddings were not lucky for Philip. As father of the bride, he was assassinated at his daughter's wedding by one of his bodyguards, leaving his son Alexander the undisputed heir at age 20. There is some belief that Alexander's mother was aware of the plot against her husband and was not opposed to becoming the widow of King Philip and the mother of King Alexander.

Claiming the throne was one thing; keeping it was another. First, Alexander had to clean house; that meant disposing of any potential rivals: family members, rival princes, and of course the rash general who had expressed his wish for a fertile marriage for the niece who had married Alexander's father.

.

That bloody duty accomplished, Alexander next turned his attentions to those conquered lands who thought that an untried youth would be easy to vanquish. The untried youth and his cavalry wasted no time in riding against the rebels. His shrewd strategy, remarkable in someone so young, brought the army to surrender. He defeated rebellious Thracians, Illyrians and Taulanti, then had to deal once again with Thebans and Athenians in revolt. Alexander had been injured during the siege of Pelium and the rumor of his death seemed credible enough, sufficiently credible to encourage Themes to revolt against their Macedonian overlords. Alexander had been relying on the presence of Macedonian troops to keep the Greeks in order, but he'd had to pull the troops when the Thracian and Illrian revolts erupted. But Alexander's military acumen was already showing its prowess as he travelled 300 miles within two weeks, miraculously bringing his army undetected to the site of the battle under the very noses of his Greek enemies.

Wary of the Macedonian's skills, Athens and Sparta

decided to play a waiting game. Thebes voted for war. Alexander was prepared to be lenient; if Thebes turned over the two men who had incited the revolt, no one would be hurt. Thebes issued a counter offer which was refused. This time, Alexander taught Thebes a lesson that was not lost on the rest of Greece; he burned the city to the ground. Those Thebans who weren't killed in battle were sold as slaves.

Alexander might have had an elite education, but when it came to warfare, he was no schoolboy. The Macedonian was intent on conquest. Next stop: Persia.

King Darius III of Persia was ready for the battle, with an army of perhaps as many as 200,000 soldiers to meet Alexander's 35,000 men (numbers are imprecise, but historians agree that Darius had a much larger force). With a tactical move that fooled the Persians into moving onto rocky terrain and away from the flat battlefield where they had the advantage, Alexander charged through the rear of the Persian army. Darius fled the battlefield. The conquest continued for several more years, but when Darius was killed in 330 BC, Alexander took his place as the Persian king. One more crown added to his collection.

He went on to conquer Egypt and Babylon. When his horse Bucephalus died in what today is Pakistan, Alexander named a city for him. Battle in India was to present a new threat in the form of war elephants. But once again, the Macedonians were triumphant. And weary.

At the Hyphasis River, the Macedonians told their ruler, their general, their companion, that they had had enough and would go no farther. Alexander was not pleased with their mutiny, and sulked in his quarters like Achilles. But they would not change their minds. When he agreed to turn back, the army broke out in cheers and shouts of joy.

The man who conquered the known world would not live long to enjoy his efforts. In June 323 BCE, he attended a banquet and along with the other guests, took part in the bouts of drinking that followed. Feeling unwell, he went to bed, his condition worsening. Realizing that he was mortally ill, his soldiers wanted to see him for one last time. Although he didn't speak, he nonetheless acknowledged with a nod or a glance the soldiers of his army as they came to him. Ten days later, with a fever sapping his strength, Alexander died at the age of 33. Given the sanitary conditions of the times, historians deduce that the cause of death might have been typhoid fever or malaria. Of course, given the political climate of the era, it might also have been poison.

Alexander had spent his adult life in conquest, acquiring lands so that he could rule them and consolidate individual nations into one empire. But his death brought an end to the dreams of lasting empire. He had married three times; his child by Roxana of Bactria, Alexander IV of Macedon, was born six months after Alexander's death. Roxana, ambitious to secure her unborn child's position as heir, had her rival wives murdered. Her efforts were futile, as Alexander IV was murdered within a few years, and the empire divided up among Alexander the Great's generals.

Why Alexander Matters

Ptolemy, one of those generals, brought Alexander's body to Alexandria, where his tomb became a favorite destination for travelers of the ancient world, including

Julius Caesar. The library at Alexandria was a great center of learning that celebrated the achievements of the Greeks and was a prized asset of the intellectual community until it was burned, centuries after Alexander's death.

Although the Greeks were conquered by the Macedonian father and son, Greek culture triumphed, and Alexander made no attempt to subdue it; he had a great regard for the sophisticated accomplishments of the Greeks. He brought his armies to the lands he conquered, but the spread of Greek culture would prove to be more enduring than his rule. Hellenistic ideals, philosophy, and learning, consolidated by the wandering conqueror, spread far across the subjugated lands. Western thought would be heavily influenced by the intellectual legacy of the Greeks. The three thousand miles of land that he claimed would become an ancient global community where trade and learning flourished.

[Excerpt from the first 2 Chapters – for complete book, please purchase on Amazon.com]